Words I Wish I Wrote

ROBERT FULGHUM

WORDS I WISH I WROTE

A COLLECTION OF WRITING THAT INSPIRED MY IDEAS

A Cliff Street Book
from HarperPerennial

A hardcover edition of this book was published in 1997 by Cliff Street Books, an imprint of HarperCollins Publishers.

First HarperPerennial edition published 1999.

Designed by David Bullen

The Library of Congress has catalogued the hardcover edition as follows:
Fulghum, Robert.
Words I wish I wrote / Robert Fulghum.—1st ed.
p. cm.
ISBN 0–06–017560–5
1. Conduct of life. 2. Fulghum, Robert—Books and reading.
I. Title.
BJ1581.2.F85 1997   97–18981

ISBN 0–06–093222–8 (pbk.)

99 00 01 02 03 ❖/RRD 10 9 8 7 6 5 4 3 2 1

To Robert L. Bernstein . . .

Publisher, mentor, and friend, on whose desk I first saw the words, "There is no limit to the good a man can do if he doesn't care who gets the credit." Former CEO of Random House and distinguished founding chairman of Human Rights Watch, the organization to which this book is also dedicated.

Human Rights Watch was founded in 1978 as Helsinki Watch, set up to support and monitor compliance with the human rights provisions of the landmark Helsinki accord with the Soviet Union. It now exposes and works to stop human rights abuses in more than seventy countries world-wide. With an experienced and dedicated staff of more than one hundred regional experts, lawyers, journalists, and linguists, plus hundreds of committed volunteers, its goal is to make governments pay a heavy price in reputation and legitimacy if they violate the rights of their people. Human Rights Watch works to end a broad range of human rights abuses, including summary executions; torture; arbitrary detention; restrictions on the freedoms of expression, association, assembly, and religion; violations of due process; and discrimination on racial, gender, ethnic, and religious grounds. It uses the standards of universal civil and political rights as embodied in international law and treaties. In every place and in every way that basic human freedoms are being violated, Human Rights Watch is at work.

All the author's net royalties from the sales of this book will be given to Human Rights Watch. Those wishing to know more about HRW can write to its New York City headquarters, 485 Fifth Avenue, New York, NY 10017–6104 or send e-mail to hrwny@hrw.org. World Wide Web site: http://www. hrw.org.

This is a gift that I have, simple, simple—a foolish
extravagant spirit, full of forms, figures, shapes, objects,
ideas, apprehensions, motions, revolutions. These
are begot in the ventricle of memory, nourished in the
womb of pia mater, and delivered upon the
mellowing of occasion.

WILLIAM SHAKESPEARE
Love's Labour's Lost, IV, ii

Contents

Begin

What do I believe? At rock bottom—about essential things—what?

And the source of those beliefs? Where did they come from?

Roots. As a child, I was taught the Christian view of life according to the Columbus Avenue Baptist Church in Waco, Texas. In college, that view was painted over first by Thoreau, then by Plato and Socratic thinking, and later by Emerson and the Unitarians. By age twenty-one, I had things figured out for myself. So I thought.

Coincidentally, in graduate school, it was required of me to write a credo—a summary statement of my convictions. The task: Locate yourself in the total scheme of things. Where do you stand? No problem. I knew.

Forty years later, I reread that thick thesis and laugh. Polysyllabic puffery. As if the depth of the meaning depended on the length of the words. Nevertheless, the sincerity of the young craftsman is apparent, even if his sanctuary was overbuilt.

Many times in the past four decades, I've reviewed and revised my credo. Sometimes as an exercise in personal growth, more often in circumstances forced by crisis. At fifty, reaching for a simplicity to match that earlier complexity, I wrote a summary essay professing that all I really need to know I learned in kindergarten. Later, I even went so far as to distill my credo into a single word: *Maybe.*

Now, in my sixtieth year, I'm curious about what lasts and what changes in this evolving credo. My reconsideration is well described in the words of playwright Lillian Hellman, in the introduction to her biographical reflection entitled *Pentimento*.

Old paint on canvas, as it ages, sometimes becomes transparent. When that happens it is possible, in some pictures, to see the original lines: a tree will show through a woman's dress, a child makes way for a dog, a large boat is no longer on an open sea. That is called pentimento because the painter "repented," changed his mind. Perhaps it would be as well to say that the old conception, replaced by a later choice, is a way of seeing and then seeing again. That is all I mean about the people in this book. The paint has aged now and I wanted to see what was there for me once, what is there for me now.

To see and then see again. And what I see now as I inspect my credo quest is this quality of pentimento. This translucent layering of belief becomes a self-portrait painted in words. There is a transparency to my accumulated writing. When I look deep beneath my declarations, I see the underlying thoughts of others. As hard as I have tried to speak in my own voice, I realize now how much of what I have said is neither original nor unique. My expressions echo and imitate the statements of others. Even *that* realization has come to others before me as they reviewed their own conclusions. Thought is forever being revived, recycled, and renewed. The great painter Matisse put it this way: "For my part I have never avoided the influence of others. I would have considered it cowardice and a lack of sincerity toward myself."

No apology, then. No regrets. My convictions have validity for me because I have experimented with the compounds of ideas of others in the laboratory of my mind. And I've tested the results in the living out of my life. At twenty-one, I had drawn an abstract map based on the evidence of others. At sixty, I have accumulated a practical guide grounded in my own experience. At twenty-one, I could discuss transportation theory with authority. At sixty, I know which bus to catch to go where, what the fare is, and how to get back home again. It is not my bus, but I know how to use it.

Look at this line of thought from another angle. Consider these questions: If your life were made into a movie, and that movie had an appropriate sound track, and I bought a CD of the music, what kind of music would it be? What mood would it leave me in when I played it? What would I recognize? Could I dance to it?

That's a set of questions I first asked myself. I have since pestered many friends with it, generating engaging conversations. The questions necessarily impose limitations: The music must fit on a single CD—choices must be made. No defense of choice is necessary. It's assumed the selections will be idiosyncratic—combining some music in the common realm with bits and pieces of melody patched together from who knows where.

The music of the sound track of a life will not be original, but it has passed into us and left its sound in the jukebox of the mind, becoming part of us. And we will likely pass it on.

In this same spirit, I've worked back through the journals and scrapbooks I've kept since I was seventeen and have chosen the words of others that can be seen in the layers underlying my credo. As with the sound track, difficult practical choices must be made; the selections must fit in a small book and have some useful meaning for others. Choosing is not easy.

Having said that, I'm led to a statement about choosing, written by Viktor Frankl in *Man's Search for Meaning*. These words shape the spirit of this book. They illuminated my thinking like a lightning strike from the moment I encountered them many years ago:

We who lived in concentration camps can remember the men who walked through the huts comforting others, giving away their last piece of bread. They may have been few in number, but they offer sufficient proof that everything can be taken from a man but one thing: the last of the human freedoms—to choose one's attitude in any given set of circumstances, to choose one's own way.

To choose one's own way. Yes. But, in so doing, I've found that others have always been this way before me. And they have spoken of the way in words I wish I had written—in language I could not improve upon. Not a discouraging realization at all, but the recognition of great companionship, and the affirming consolation that becomes a life preserver against loneliness.

So then. Here is a compilation of a part of my personal resources. Beneath the house of my life are foundation stones laid by others. Within the walls of the house of my life is a framework constructed by those who have lived before me. This book is a credo pentimento: the exhibition of the ideas underlying my living and thinking as I have gone about choosing my own way.

Choose

Biography.

My generation wasn't labeled Lost, or Hip, or Yup. Mine was Beat. Arriving in San Francisco in 1958, direct from central Texas, I shed the suit and tie of the IBM career I fled, stored the jeans and cowboy boots of my adolescence, and took up the bohemian style of the Beatnik: black turtleneck sweater, rumpled corduroy trousers, leather sandals, and French beret. A beard was desirable, but at twenty-one my facial follicles were capable of sprouting only a frazzled mustache.

We Beatniks lived off a mental gruel of bogus Buddhism, existential angst, apocalyptic cynicism, bitter coffee, cheap wine, narcissistic poetry, and the free-form jazz being served up in the coffeehouse milieu of San Francisco's North Beach area. It seemed painfully profound at the time.

Ginsberg's *Howl* was the anthem of the era. The City Lights bookstore was the source for all brands of the contraband thinking of the Beat Generation. The required reading was Kerouac and Sartre, Baudelaire and Kierkegaard, Beckett and Ionesco, and the Zen masters of Japan. All of Bergman's films were must-see. And you were nothing if you didn't groove to Coltrane and Miles.

The truth: I was a weekend Beatnik. I had a wife and child and graduate school obligations in Berkeley. In that world, I studied theology and philosophy in seminars during the day, worked nights as a bartender, and once a week as an intern in a mental hospital. I studied on the run and wrote papers in the small hours of the morning. A hard, heavy load. It was in that weekday world that I was literally beat much of the time.

Out of choice and necessity, I wallowed around in the muddy bottom of the valley of the absurd. I reveled in the public image of living on the edge of desperation, while secretly loathing the reality of my life. I was scared, confused, and angry. Long hours were spent obsessed with dying and death—both my own and the death of the world through a nuclear apocalypse. Behind the costume, mask, and pose of fashionable angst, I lived a real life in genuine despair. I was more than Beat. I was Overwhelmed.

In that winter of 1958–59, I began reading the novels and essays of Albert Camus, who had won the Nobel Prize for Literature in 1957. He had experienced much harsher circumstances than I. He had stood at the edge of a much deeper abyss—had looked down with open eyes. And he had stepped back from the edge.

Camus confirmed the absurdity of the human condition, but he also affirmed the ability to choose to assert one's humanity by rebelling against that absurdity. Camus chose to defy his fate. He chose life over death. Chose YES instead of NO. He chose climbing the mountain of existence over sliding into the chasm of oblivion.

This idea of choosing—of being free to choose—was a life preserver I could cling to. His experiences validated my own. His footsteps in the sands of time gave me a direction to follow. Camus's YES! has remained visible in my life and in my credo. His books hold an honored place as rock-solid foundation references for my thinking. My copies of his journals are worn and dog-eared from use.

I've actively looked for and saved confirming statements from other yea-sayers, recorded them in my journals, and restated them in my credo. They all confirm that the elemental question of existence is asked daily and always: Life or Death? Yes or No?

As for me, count me in the determined company of those who choose Life and Yes, no matter what.

Judging whether life is or is not worth living amounts to answering the fundamental question of philosophy. All the rest—whether or not the world has three dimensions, whether the mind has nine or twelve categories—comes afterward. These are games; one must first answer.

ALBERT CAMUS

In the midst of winter, I found there was within me,
an invincible summer.

ALBERT CAMUS

These, then, are my last words to you: Be not afraid of life. Believe that life *is* worth living, and your belief will help create the fact. The "scientific proof" that you are right may not be clear before the day of judgment (or some stage of being which that expression may serve to symbolize) is reached. But the faithful fighters of the hour, or the beings that then and there will represent them, may then turn to the faint-hearted, who here decline to go on, with words like those with which Henry IV greeted the tardy Crillon after a great battle had been gained: "Hang yourself, brave Crillon! we fought at Arques, and you were not there."

WILLIAM JAMES

The Will to Believe

This is the world: the lying likeness of
Our strips of stuff that tatter as we move
Loving and being loth;
The dream that kicks the buried from their sack
And lets their trash be honoured as the quick.
This is the world. Have faith.

For we shall be a shouter like the cock,
Blowing the old dead back; our shots shall smack
The image from the plates;
And we shall be fit fellows for a life,
And who remain shall flower as they love,
Praise to our faring hearts.

DYLAN THOMAS
"Our Eunuch Dreams"

The great thing about suicide is that it's not one of those things you have to do now or you lose your chance. I mean, you can always do it *later*.

HARVEY FIERSTEIN

After the final no there comes a yes
And on that yes the future world depends.
No was the night. Yes is this present sun.

WALLACE STEVENS
"The Well Dressed Man with a Beard"

17

I know we often lose, and that the death or destruction of another is infinitely more real and unbearable than one's own. I think I know how many times one has to start again, and how often one feels that one cannot start again. And yet, on pain of death, one can never remain where one is. . . . It is a mighty heritage, it is the human heritage, and it is all there is to trust. . . . This is why one must say Yes to life and embrace it wherever it is found—and it is found in terrible places; nevertheless, there it is; and if the father can say, "Yes, Lord," the child can learn that most difficult of words, *Amen.*

JAMES BALDWIN
Nothing Personal

Annotations

(Each chapter of this book is a self-contained unit and not directly connected in mood or subject matter with the next chapter. I've not given an annotation for every quote—only where I've something personal to add or where a little more information helps justify the place of the quotation in the book.)

Albert Camus is identified with French existentialism, but his courageous humanism sets him apart from Sartre and others. While I give away many books after reading them, I have kept the works of Camus: his novels, *The Stranger, The Plague, The Fall;* his essays, including "The Myth of Sisyphus"; and all his published journals. He's on my list of authors I wish I had known personally.

William James—philosopher, psychologist, and brother of novelist Henry James—wrote three of the books that most influenced my thinking about religion and philosophy: *The Will to Believe, The Varieties of Religious Experience,* and *Pragmatism.* They are the books I've most often given as gifts to those trying to apply intelligence to matters of faith.

On that same list of authors I wish I had known is Dylan Thomas, my favorite poet. His single volume of collected poems has often been taken along on backpacking trips to be read aloud to companions around an evening fire. Listening to his recording of *A Child's Christmas in Wales* is an annual winter's treat for me.

Harvey Fierstein is a Tony Award–winning Broadway playwright and actor. The film made from his play *Torch*

Song Trilogy did more for my understanding of what it means to be gay than anything I've read or experienced. A big bear of a man with a deep, gravelly voice, Fierstein's poignant wit is wise and audacious, especially when delivered while he's dressed in full drag.

Pulitzer Prize–winning poet WALLACE STEVENS, a lawyer by training, was for forty years associated with innovations in insurance while with the Hartford Accident and Indemnity Company. In addition to his *Collected Poems,* I value the selections from his journals, published as *Souvenirs and Prophecies.*

JAMES BALDWIN was the first black author I read—in 1955. His novel *Go Tell It on the Mountain* and his book of essays *The Fire Next Time* are just two of the many books he wrote that revised my racial views and shaped my thinking about civil rights. His writing drew me into the work of the movement toward integration as much as the words of Martin Luther King, Jr.

Possible

Books on theology and philosophy are not on the table alongside the chair where I sit and read. Haven't been for a long time. And that's odd, since these topics were at the core of my reading and thinking for three decades. Now, looking at the shelf where I keep my permanent collection of books, I see I've managed to sort through and give to a public library almost all my volumes of theology and philosophy. They represent guides to mental mountain ranges I've slogged my way across. I don't plan to go back that way. The woods there are too thick, the air too thin, and being snowed in there by blizzards of unrelenting analytical thought is depressing.

What do I read now? Astronomy. And not so much read it as consider the pictures. The most profound theological and philosophical statements being made these days are in the photographs taken from the Hubble Space Telescope. And the most jarring picture is the Hubble Deep Field. It's a ten-day exposure, covering an area of the sky no larger than a grain of sand held at arm's length.

I'm looking at this photograph as I write. It hangs on the wall just above and behind my computer screen. In a cosmic sea of black space whirl galaxies beyond counting, eight to ten billion light-years away. Their light headed our direction long before the Earth existed. These galaxies are remarkably dissimilar: spiral ones and barred ones, elliptical, interacting, and—get this—forty percent of them are "peculiar." In the language of astronomy, that means these galaxies don't fit any standard classification scheme. Unseen before. Unexplainable now. Perhaps forever incomprehensible. I gaze at the Hubble Deep Field photograph in awe.

If this isn't enough, astronomers have extrapolated the information about this small window in the sky to estimate that there are more than fifty billion galaxies out there. Fifty billion.

The view from much closer in is likewise astonishing to me. Last night I saw the French film *Microcosmos.* Lots of sex and violence and beauty—even laughs. Dinosaurlike creatures procreating and eating and being eaten. Sounds like the usual film fare these days, but all the stars of the show were insects. Using the most sophisticated microphotographic technology, the film gives a close-up view of a day in the life of the majority of the creatures of the Earth, as unseen before.

(My wife said she was afraid to go outside after seeing the film. So I didn't show her the book I bought showing photographs of the microscopic mites that live on our faces and infest our bed. These mites, furthermore, have even more microscopic mites on them. They live off human skin. And they are crawling around on your nose as you read this.)

I'm not even going to mention quarks and black holes or bacteria and viruses in this rundown of mind-bending information. Stars and bugs are enough to suggest my point of view.

To paraphrase Lord Haldane, the pioneering British scientist, it's clear to me that the universe is not only more formidably fantastic than we imagine, it is more fantastic than we ever *can* imagine. The philosophies and cosmologies and gods we have created are all far too small.

Furthermore, human affairs are part of this unimaginable sea of what may be. As in the sky above our heads and the ground beneath our feet, so also in the world of daily experience all around us. Everything and anything imaginable is possible. And everything and anything beyond that.

Infinite possibility in all things is a certainty.

That pretty much covers theology and philosophy for me.

If we knew we were on the right road, having to leave it would mean endless despair. But we are on a road that only leads to a second one and then to a third one and so forth. And the real highway will not be sighted for a long, long time, perhaps never. So we drift in doubt. But also in an unbelievable beautiful diversity. Thus the accomplishment of hopes remains an always unexpected miracle. But in compensation, the miracle remains forever possible.

FRANZ KAFKA
Diaries

Come now! . . . Were everything clear, all would seem to you vain. Your boredom would populate a shadowless universe with an impassive life made up of unleavened souls. But a measure of disquiet is a divine gift. The hope which, in your eyes, shines on a dark threshold does not have its basis in an overly certain world.

MARCEL PROUST
By Way of Sainte-Beuve

. . . have patience with everything that remains unsolved in your heart. Try to love the *questions themselves,* like locked rooms and like books written in a foreign language. Do not now look for the answers. They cannot now be given to you because you could not live them. It is a question of experiencing everything. At present you need to *live* the question. Perhaps you will gradually, without even noticing it, find yourself experiencing the answer, some distant day.

RAINER MARIA RILKE

Letters to a Young Poet

Kilgore Trout once wrote a short story which was a dialogue between two pieces of yeast. They were discussing the possible purposes of life as they ate sugar and suffocated in their own excrement. Because of their limited intelligence, they never came close to guessing that they were making champagne.

KURT VONNEGUT, JR.
Breakfast of Champions

People know what they do;
they frequently know why they do what they do;
but what they don't know
is what what they do does.

MICHEL FOUCAULT
The Order of Things

Between the finite limitations of the five senses
and the endless yearnings of man for the beyond
the people hold to the humdrum bidding of work and food
while reaching out when it comes their way
for lights beyond the prisms of the five senses,
for keepsakes lasting beyond any hunger or death.
    This reaching is alive.
The panderers and liars have violated and smutted it.
    Yet this reaching is alive yet
      for lights and keepsakes.

CARL SANDBURG
The People, Yes

Man is neither unique nor central nor necessarily here to stay. But he is a product of circumstances special to the point of disbelief. And if man in his current predicament seeks a fair mystique to see him through, then I can only suggest that he consider his genes. For they are marked. They are graven by luck beyond explanation. They are stamped by forces that we shall never know. But even so, in the hieroglyph of the human emergence certain symbols must stand for all to read: Change is the elixir of the human circumstance, and acceptance of challenge the way of our kind. We are bad-weather animals, disaster's fairest children. For the soundest of evolutionary reasons man appears at his best when times are worst.

ROBERT ARDREY
"Cain's Children," in *African Genesis*

To the question whether I am a pessimist or an optimist,
I answer that my knowledge is pessimistic, but my willing
and hoping are optimistic.

ALBERT SCHWEITZER

(From an interview)

*(When I was a senior in high school, the librarian gave me a biography of
Schweitzer, which captured my imagination. I read everything I could find about
him and studied up on Africa as if I were leaving on the next boat. When I was
introduced to his renditions of Bach organ music, at about the same time I became
a minister, it became my ritual to write my sermons on Saturday evening while lis-
tening to Schweitzer play.)*

No pessimist ever discovered the secrets of the stars, or sailed to an uncharted land, or opened a new heaven to the human spirit.

HELEN KELLER

You can count how many seeds are in the apple, but not how many apples are in the seed.

KEN KERSEY

The universe is infinite in every direction.

Annotations

When FRANZ KAFKA died of tuberculosis at age forty-one, he left three unfinished novels and all his papers and diaries to his friend Max Brod, with instructions that they be burned. Instead, Brod edited and published almost all of the material. Though the novels are difficult and depressing reading, the diaries contain occasional flashes of appealing optimism.

MARCEL PROUST is best known for his monumental masterpiece, *Remembrance of Things Past,* which took me three years to finish. I found *By Way of Sainte-Beuve* a more useful and accessible insight into Proust's thought. This work is an exploratory preparation for his great novel.

Though primarily thought of as the finest poet writing in German in the twentieth century, RAINER MARIA RILKE wrote prose that is equally eloquent. I've often passed on his *Letters to a Young Poet* to young people seeking a life in the arts.

KURT VONNEGUT, JR. doesn't really have a category in literature—his major works are a mix of narrative fiction, philosophy, history, science fiction, humor, and a gift for aphoristic commentary. *Cat's Cradle* and *Slaughterhouse Five* are the works I most admire. Both of my copies of these books are heavily underlined. His joyful cynicism and quirky humor spark my thinking.

MICHEL FOUCAULT, modern French philosopher and essayist, served the culture of his times by being an agent provocateur in the realm of the history of ideas. His work is important to structuralism, a complex revision of how meaning is determined in literature, as well as in anthropology, linguistics, and mathematics.

The People, Yes by CARL SANDBURG is my favorite American long poem. Underneath his writing can be seen the thought and style and interests of Walt Whitman. Not only successful as a poet, Sandburg wrote a substantial biographical study of Abraham Lincoln, collected American folklore and folk songs, wrote children's stories, and served as secretary to the first socialist mayor of the city of Milwaukee.

While ROBERT ARDREY wrote plays, screenplays, and novels, I value most his three books of speculative popular science: *African Genesis, The Territorial Imperative,* and *The Social Contract.*

ALBERT SCHWEITZER was a world-class theologian, philosopher, and musician—and a medical doctor on top of that. How astonishing that he spent most of his life as a medical missionary in what was then French Equatorial Africa. His philosophy of "reverence for life" was woven into my philosophy in my twenties when I read his book *Out of My Life and Thought.* His *Quest for the Historical Jesus* still makes sense to me, though it was written in 1906. He was awarded the Nobel Peace Prize in 1952.

Completely blind and deaf by age two, HELEN KELLER was educated by her lifelong companion, Anne Sullivan Macy, who also taught her how to speak. Despite her disabilities, Keller graduated cum laude from Radcliffe College in 1904. Her six autobiographical books tell an astonishing story, part of which was dramatized in the award-winning Broadway play and film *The Miracle Worker.* Helen Keller opened a whole new era in the way blind and deaf people were perceived, treated, and educated.

KEN KERSEY was a jazz pianist, one of the most advanced swing pianists in his day—the early 1940s in New York.

FREEMAN DYSON's field is physics, but his avocation is studying the impact of science on civilization. He is a member of the faculty of the Institute of Advance Study at Princeton.

There are three fine astronomy magazines: *Sky and Telescope, Astronomy,* and *Sky News.* I find them readily available at newstands and by mail. I buy all three, because the content and points of view vary. As with other contemporary science magazines, they reach out to all levels of amateur interest and provide access to almost anything you want to know or buy in the field. Not a month goes by that I'm not stunned by what I read and see in these magazines.

My own interests are usually satisfied by very high-powered binoculars and a guide for the simpleminded to the most obvious sights in the sky. As I say, it's not the science that intrigues me—it's the magnifying implications for my philosophy and theology.

Journey

Debts. Big debts.

Owed by me to an English cavalry officer, an American pencil maker, a Greek bard, an Austro-Hungarian poet, a Colombian novelist, an Alexandrian clerk, and a Japanese printmaker. In this essay, I will speak of two and elaborate on the others in the annotations at the end of the chapter.

To begin with, the English general.

Robert Stephenson Smyth Baden-Powell, First Baron of Gilwell, was born in 1857 and died in 1941. If that information doesn't ring any bells with you, I'm not surprised. Though my life at an early age was indelibly influenced by him, I didn't know much about him myself until I read a biography many years later. Lieutenant General Baden-Powell founded the Boy Scouts in England in 1908.

The first uniform I ever wore was the blue-and-yellow ensemble of a Cub Scout. Age seven. I still have the yellow bandanna, navy blue cap, and shirt. Part of the pleasure was the quasi-military drill of marching with my troop in town parades. I think that's why I joined. But I remained to become first a full Scout and then an Explorer Scout for the next ten years because I wanted to go camping.

Camping was not a family affair. My mother was a delicate, tubercular woman who didn't even like picnics. My father had no interest in doing for fun what he did in his own childhood as a necessity while growing up in near-poverty in the deep piney-woods of east Texas. Roughing it in the field was something he had spent his life getting away from.

Going off on weekend hiking trips with the Scouts was

more than an experience in camping in the woods for me. It was a legitimized form of regularly running away from home. Mine was a bitterly contentious family. The details need not be recounted here. Suffice it to say that camping out on weekends and during vacations was an escape from unhappiness. The outdoors became my refuge. And for fifty years it has remained so. Hiking, backpacking, canoeing, river rafting, mountain climbing, cross-country skiing, and kayaking—all these hold the finest memories of the best of times, to this day. When my children were young, we lived for several summers under canvas in the mountains of eastern British Columbia. It may have been the happiest time of our lives for all of us.

Whether I am out with a group of friends or alone, one uncommon companion always accompanies me. Although he died on May 6, 1862, his thoughts remain very much alive and available. I met him on the first day of my first English class in college. The assignment: Read selections from *Walden,* by Henry David Thoreau. I had never heard of him or his book. Nor did I have much interest in pencil makers who lived by ponds in New England. But I stayed up all night reading *Walden.*

To this day I've never gone to the woods without Henry for company. As I write, there is on the desk before me a much-battered volume of *Walden.* Its fragility has finally retired it from outdoor use. On its flyleaf are fifteen dates noting complete rereadings. Its pages are underlined and annotated. Between pages, I find such keepsakes as pressed wildflowers, autumn leaves, spring grasses, and feathers. Smudges of soot and dirt, stains of bacon grease, and spots of rain are also keepsakes—some marked with exact place and date and time. Its replacement copy is rapidly taking on the same character.

In going out and coming back, I've taken Henry along—not only to the outdoors, but on my journeys of the spirit, taken to transact private business with myself. That's the same reason Henry gives for going to Walden in the first place.

I went to the woods because I wished to live deliberately, to front only the essential facts of life, and see if I could not learn what it had to teach, and not, when I came to die, discover that I had not lived. I did not wish to live what was not life, living is so dear; nor did I wish to practice resignation, unless it was quite necessary. I wanted to live deep and suck out all the marrow of life, to live so sturdily and Spartan-like as to put to rout all that was not life, to cut a broad swath and shave close, to drive life into a corner, and reduce it to its lowest terms, and, if it proved to be mean, why then to get the whole and genuine meanness of it, and publish its meanness to the world; or if it were sublime, to know it by experience, and be able to give a true account of it in my next excursion.

HENRY DAVID THOREAU
Walden

I left the woods for as good a reason as I went th
Perhaps it seemed to me that I had several more
live, and could not spare any more time for that one. . . .
I learned this, at least, by my experiment; that if one
advances confidently in the direction of his dreams, and
endeavors to live the life which he has imagined, he will
meet with a success unexpected in common hours.

HENRY DAVID THOREAU
Walden

. . . he allowed himself to be swayed by his conviction that human beings are not born once and for all on the day their mothers give birth to them, but that life obliges them over and over again to give birth to themselves.

GABRIEL GARCÍA MÁRQUEZ
Love in the Time of Cholera

Ithaca

When you start on your journey to Ithaca,
then pray that the road is long,
full of adventure, full of knowledge,
Do not fear the Lestrygonians
and the Cyclopes and the angry Poseidon.
You will never meet such as these on your path,
if your thoughts remain lofty, if a fine
emotion touches your body and your spirit.
You will never meet the Lestrygonians,
the Cyclopes and the fierce Poseidon,
if you do not carry them within your soul,
if your soul does not raise them up before you.

Then pray that the road is long.
That the summer mornings are many,
that you will enter ports seen for the first time
with such pleasure, with such joy!
Stop at Phoenician markets,
and purchase fine merchandise,
mother-of-pearl and corals, amber and ebony,
and pleasurable perfumes of all kinds,
visit hosts of Egyptian cities,
to learn and learn from those who have knowledge.

Always keep Ithaca fixed in your mind.
To arrive there is your ultimate goal.
But do not hurry the voyage at all.
It is better to let it last for long years;

and even to anchor at the isle when you are old,
rich with all that you have gained on the way,
not expecting that Ithaca will offer you riches.

Ithaca has given you the beautiful voyage.
Without her you would never have taken the road.
But she has nothing more to give you.

And if you find her poor, Ithaca has not defrauded you.
With the great wisdom you have gained, with so much
    experience,
you must surely have understood by then what Ithacas
    mean.

C. P. CAVAFY
Complete Poems

(Ithaca was the home of Odysseus, whose journey is described in Homer's Odyssey.
*Cavafy's poem is one of the great comments on the value of the going versus the get-
ting there, the journey of living versus the ultimate destination, death.)*

For poems are not, as people think, simply emotions
(one has emotions early enough)—they are experiences.
For the sake of a single poem, you must see many cities,
many people and Things, you must understand animals,
must feel how birds fly, and know the gesture which small
flowers make when they open in the morning. You must be
able to think back to streets in unknown neighborhoods,
to unexpected encounters, and to partings you had long
seen coming; to days of childhood whose mystery is still
unexplained, to parents whom you had to hurt when they
brought in a joy and you didn't pick it up (it was a joy
meant for somebody else—); to childhood illnesses that
began so strangely with so many profound and difficult
transformations, to days in quiet, restrained rooms and to
mornings by the sea, to the sea itself, to seas, to nights of
travel that rushed along high overhead and went flying
with all the stars,—and it is still not enough to be able to
think of all that. You must have memories of many nights
of love, each one different from all the others, memories
of women screaming in labor, and of light, pale, sleeping
girls who have just given birth and are closing again. But
you must also have been beside the dying, must have sat
beside the dead in the room with the open window and
the scattered noises. And it is not yet enough to have
memories. You must be able to forget them when they are
many, and you must have the immense patience to wait
until they return. For the memories themselves are not
important. Only when they have changed into our very
blood, into glance and gesture, and are nameless, no

longer to be distinguished from ourselves—only then can it happen that in some very rare hour the first word of a poem arises in their midst and goes forth from them.

RAINER MARIA RILKE
"The Notebooks of Malte Laurids Brigge"

Once, I remembered, I had detached a chrysalis from the trunk of an olive tree and placed it in my palm. Inside the transparent coating I discerned a living thing. It was moving. The hidden process must have reached its terminus; the future, still-enslaved butterfly was waiting with silent tremors for the sacred hour when it would emerge into the sunlight. It was not in a hurry. Having confidence in the light, the warm air, in God's eternal law, it was waiting.

But I was in a hurry. I wanted to see the miracle hatch before me as soon as possible, wanted to see how the body surges out of its tomb and shroud to become a soul. Bending over, I began to blow my warm breath over the chrysalis, and behold! a slit soon incised itself on the chrysalis's back, the entire shroud gradually split from top to bottom, and the immature, bright green butterfly appeared, still tightly locked together, its wings twisted, its legs glued to its abdomen. It squirmed gently and kept coming more and more to life beneath my warm, persistent breath. One wing as pale as a budding poplar leaf disengaged itself from the body and began to palpitate, struggling to unfold along its entire length, but in vain. It stayed half opened, shriveled. Soon the other wing moved as well, toiled in its own right to stretch, was unable to, and remained half unfolded and trembling. I, with a human being's effrontery, continued to lean over and blow my warm exhalation upon the maimed wings, but they had ceased to move now and had drooped down, as stiff and lifeless as stone.

I felt sick at heart. Because of my hurry, because I had dared to transgress an eternal law, I had killed the butterfly. In my hand I held a carcass. Years and years have passed, but that butterfly's weightless carcass has weighed heavily on my conscience ever since.

NIKOS KAZANTZAKIS
Report to Greco

Ever since the age of six I have had a mania for drawing the forms of objects. Towards the age of fifty I published a very large number of drawings, but I am dissatisfied with everything which I produced before the age of seventy. It was at the age of seventy-three I nearly mastered the real nature and form of birds, fish, plants, etcetera. Consequently, at the age of eighty, I shall have got to the bottom of things; at one hundred I shall have attained a decidedly higher level which I cannot define, and at the age of one hundred and ten every dot and every line from my brush will be alive. I call on those who may live as long as I to see if I keep my word.

Signed, formerly Hokusai,
now the Painting-Crazy Old Man

(These words are tacked to the wall over the sink in my studio, where I wash out my brushes after working on my paintings, while reflecting on what I've accomplished on canvas for the day. Hokusai, the great Japanese master printmaker, influenced the French Impressionists, from whom I in turn draw inspiration for my own art. Hokusai's attitude was that artistic growth was continuous and his best work was always ahead of him. It proved to be the case for him; he was still producing art at his death at ninety. May it be so for me.)

Annotations

My favorite version of THOREAU's *Walden* has a foreword by Edward Abbey, written as Abbey himself reread *Walden* on a trip down the Green and Colorado Rivers in Utah. The version gives you two fine companions, Ed and Henry. (It is published by Gibbs Smith, Salt Lake City, 1981.) If you enjoy Thoreau, I recommend owning his complete journals, which were the sources of his books. (Published in two volumes by Dover Publications, New York, 1962.) And read Edward Abbey's journal, *Desert Solitaire,* or his novel, *The Monkey Wrench Gang,* both of which have been influential in the movement to preserve wilderness.

GABRIEL GARCÍA MÁRQUEZ, Nobel Prize winner in literature, needs no praise from me. How I wish I could read him in Spanish. *Love in the Time of Cholera* is on my list of Best Novels—both for story and craftsmanship—and it's on my shelf of novels to be kept and read again and again.

CONSTANTINE CAVAFY, a Greek, was born and lived out his life in Alexandria, Egypt, writing poetry while working lifelong as a clerk in the ministry of irrigation. Championed by E. M. Forster, Cavafy also appears as a fixture in Lawrence Durrell's Alexandria Quartet, four more novels that sit on my keep-and-read-again-and-again shelf.

With the exception of Hokusai, all the authors in this section had an education in Western classical literature—which means they read and were influenced by Homer. NIKOS KAZANTZAKIS wrote a sequel to Homer's *Odyssey* and lived out a lifelong odyssey of his own, adventuring into many countries, cultures, religions, and political theories, borrowing from all as he chose his way. In addition to

Zorba the Greek, four other major works are important to me: *Symposium, Report to Greco, Freedom and Death,* and *The Last Temptation of Christ.*

As for HOKUSAI, my appreciation for his life and work may be gauged by my having paid my respects at his grave at the Seikyo temple in Tokyo the first time I visited Japan. There are many fine volumes of his famous prints, but my favorite collection of his work is *The Hokusai Sketch-Books,* containing many of his endlessly lively drawings. The author, James A. Michener, himself a prodigious talent, provides a personal and scholarly commentary on the drawings that is as fascinating as the sketches themselves. (Published by Charles E. Tuttle, Vermont and Tokyo, 1989.)

Simplify

If Occam had a razor, then Korzybski had a cleaver.

William of Occam (1285–1349), known as Doctor Invincibilis, was a Franciscan theologian/philosopher who is most remembered for his famous principle of economy in logic: "Entities [meaning assumptions used to explain phenomena] should not be multiplied beyond what is needed." This dictum, ever after called "Occam's razor," remains an admonition to all thinkers that truth is best when simply stated. Occam insisted that verbiage should be shaved away until the simplest truth stands free. He recognized that language is metaphor for truth, not a chemical process by which truth is extracted.

Occam's razor may be sharpened further into a more familiar modern formula: K.I.S.S.—Keep It Simple, Stupid. I latched onto Occam's razor while studying philosophy in college. It has remained in my mental tool kit ever since.

About Korzybski's cleaver. Alfred Korzybski (1879–1950), founder of modern semantics and provider of another small lifeboat for me in the deep sea of philosophy, said, "The map is not the territory." Meaning that the abstractions (words, graphs, charts) about reality are only symbols of the real world and are not to be confused with the world itself. There is no rain or traffic delay or pothole on road maps. Words are not the things for which they stand; that is, the word *dog* is not a dog, it is a word. And there is no universally correct word for a dog, as you will discover if you try to buy one in a non English-speaking country. Likewise, *God* is not the correct name of the ultimate mystery of the universe—it is a word, one of many metaphors for that which is beyond names.

We speak poetry, not substance.

Not to understand this is to risk great evil. To this day, for example, people war with each other over the correctness of creedal formulations, condemn each other over which words are obscene, and alienate each other over the labeling of one another. Korzybski's cleaver is a tool used to sharply divide words from reality.

Both Occam and Korzybski would have appreciated K.I.S.S. The power of K.I.S.S. is seen by most of us every day. Bumper stickers, graffiti, and aphorisms are potent because of their simplicity. It's not what they say, but what they suggest and provoke that makes them effective. How much explication do the following simple statements really need?

Help get the U.S. out of North America.

Read the small print and see the big picture.

Sex is a misdemeanor. The more I miss, the meaner I get.

As with language, so with life: Less is often more. The quality of life is marked by what you can do without and still do well. The best things in life aren't. Simplify. Thoreau subscribed to this line of thinking. So did Buddha, Lao-tzu, and Jesus. Possession is nine tenths of our flaw.

I once made a list of what I personally needed to have a sense of well-being. The list isn't long, and the items aren't expensive or quantified. Ten items:

Health—physical, mental, spiritual

Food—basic sustenance

Shelter—a warm, dry place to sleep

Income—more in than out

Love—the companionship of family and friends

Adventure—for mind and body

Civil rights—freedom

Education—knowledge and the ongoing chance to learn

Work—meaningful work

Chocolate

Everyone says that my way of life is the way of a simpleton.
Being largely the way of a simpleton is what makes it
worth while.
If it were not the way of a simpleton
It would long ago have been worthless,
These possessions of a simpleton being the three I choose
And cherish:
    To care,
    To be fair,
    To be humble.
When a man cares he is unafraid,
When he is fair he leaves enough for others,
When he is humble he can grow;
Whereas if, like men of today, he be bold without caring,
Self-indulgent without sharing,
Self-important without shame,
He is dead.
The invincible shield
Of caring
Is a weapon from the sky
Against being dead.

> LAO-TZU
> *Tao Te Ching*

I am done
with great things and big things
with great institutions and big
success.
And I am for
those tiny, invisible, molecular
moral forces
that work from individual to individual
through the crannies of the world
like so many rootlets
or like capillary oozing of
water
yet which, if you give them time
will rend
the hardest monuments of man's
pride.

WILLIAM JAMES
From a letter to
Mrs. Henry Whitman, June 7, 1899

(As with many other inspiring quotations, this was found in Pete Seeger's column in Sing Out *magazine. It's no surprise that Pete saw singable poetry in the prose of William James's correspondence.)*

The society which scorns excellence in plumbing because plumbing is a humble activity, and tolerates shoddiness in philosophy because philosophy is an exalted activity, will have neither good plumbing nor good philosophy. Neither its pipes nor its theories will hold water.

JOHN W. GARDNER

A New York plumber of foreign extraction with a limited command of English wrote the National Bureau of Standards and said he found that hydrochloric acid quickly opened drainage pipes when they got clogged and asked if it was a good thing to use.

A Bureau scientist replied:

"The efficacy of hydrochloric acid is indisputable, but the corrosive residue is incompatible with metallic permanence."

The plumber wrote back thanking the Bureau for telling him the method was all right. The scientist was a little disturbed and showed the correspondence to his boss, another scientist. The latter wrote the plumber:

"We cannot assume responsibility for the production of toxic and noxious residue with hydrochloric acid and suggest you use an alternative procedure."

The plumber wrote back that he agreed with the Bureau—hydrochloric acid works fine. A top scientist—boss of the first two—broke the impasse by tearing himself loose from technical terminology and writing this letter:

"Don't use hydrochloric acid. It eats hell out of the pipes."

F. F. COLTON
Scientific Monthly, 1949

(I've had this item in my files since 1959. Many's the time I've thought about it and used it as an admonition about plain speaking.)

And came forth like Venus from an ocean of
heat waves, morning in his pockets and the buckets in
    his hands
he emerged from the grey shed, tobacco and wind
pursed together in song from his tight lips he gathered day
and went out to cast wheat before swine. And in
his mind he sang songs and thought thoughts, images
    of clay
and heat, wind and sweat, dreams of silver and
visions of green earth twisting the cups of his mind
he crossed his fence of wire, the south Utah steppes
bending the air into corners of sky he entered
the yard to feed his swine. And his pigs, they come.

DAVID LEE

The Porcine Canticles

*(It would take a remarkable man to see beauty in the life and times of a pig farmer.
David Lee is such a man—poet, teacher, raconteur, and all-around fine human
being. And he crowns his elegant poems with laughter. Many's the time I've given
Lee's poetry to someone, promising to buy them any book of their choice if they don't
treasure these pig-farming poems. No takers.)*

There is really nothing you must be.
And there is nothing you must do.
There is really nothing you must have.
And there is nothing you must know.
There is really nothing you must become.
However. It helps to understand that fire burns,
 and when it rains, the earth gets wet . . .

MANABU FOLJAMAKIS

(The essence of this statement was translated for me into English from a Japanese scroll hanging in a foyer of a Zen Buddhist temple in Kyoto: One may do as one will, but one must take the consequences. I have rephrased it, added to it, used it in my art and life as if it were my own. It exists in its present form as an observation by a character in an unfinished novel. Manabu is my wife's grandfather's name and Foljamakis is a Greek twist on my own last name.)

The cobra will bite you whether you call it cobra
or Mr. Cobra.

INDIAN PROVERB

Annotations

The *Tao Te Ching (Book of the Way),* has come down to us from China in the sixth century B.C. We know little of its author, LAO-TZU, though there is a myth about him I like: It is said he wanted to leave his country, to go away to die. He was not permitted to go unless he left everything he had that was valuable. He wrote eighty-one short wisdom statements and disappeared.

JOHN W. GARDNER is a writer and educator who served as President of the Carnegie Foundation for the Advancement of Teaching (1955–65) and as Secretary of the United States Department of Health Education and Welfare (1965–68). He was also a member of President Kennedy's and President Johnson's Task Force on Education. He is the author of a number of books, including his own collection, *Quotations of Wit and Wisdom,* which he published with his daughter (W. W. Norton & Company).

In addition to *The Porcine Chronicles,* DAVID LEE has written *Day's Work, My Town,* and *Driving and Drinking.* The poet laureate of the state of Utah, he is published by Copper Canyon Press. He's as good a companion in person as he is in print, with a profound range of literature at his command. Not surprising, since he is the chairman of the Department of Language and Literature at Southern Utah State College.

Praxis

Praxis: *Activity* as opposed to *theory*.

The older I get, the less attention I pay to what people say or think or hope. I notice what they do, how they live, and what they work for.

There is an unresolved argument in the arts and in politics over whether one's words are to be judged with regard to one's life. I come down on the side of integrity: The life validates or invalidates the words.

Oratory is empty if it has not been field-tested on the battlefield of experience. And I have little use for those who write beautifully and live sordidly; or those who withdraw from the world and issue instructions for how to live in it; or priesthoods that deny the realities of the flesh but wish to control the appetites and activities of those who live as whole human beings. If you don't play the game, you can't know enough to make the rules. If you are not engaged in the sweaty work of the world, you should not be in charge of the deodorant concession. And if you cannot find a way to aid progress in human affairs, then know that the smirking cynicism of the sideline critic is a form of plague—and to be one of those is to be a carrier of death instead of a preserver of life.

Strong words? Yes, and deeply felt.

The closest I ever come to angry violence is in the presence of someone who says he will not even bother to vote because it doesn't make any difference. I saw a bumper sticker on the back of an old Buick: "If voting really changed anything, it would be illegal." I felt like giving the driver a bumper bang from behind.

He's typical of those who have a shallow view of history—those who don't understand that nobody has a right to ride on the bus without making some contribution to the cost of the journey. They don't respect the fact that somebody else paid the price to build the vehicle of civilization in the first place. They owe. We owe. It's a moral obligation to participate in the work of society. If you take from the pot, you must put into the pot. Even those who have no money can sing and keep the driver of the bus awake and hopeful.

It has been said that the hottest places in Hell are reserved for those who, in times of moral crisis, maintain their neutrality. And I say the moral crisis of the times is continuous. Knowing and understanding and being are not enough. One must do. To gain the world and give nothing to it is to lose your soul.

In the words of Norman Cousins, "The tragedy of life is not death, but what we let die inside us while we live."

I realize that it is not my role to transform either the world or man: I have neither sufficient virtue nor insight for that. But it may be to serve, in my place, those few values without which even a transformed world would not be worth living in, and man, even if "new," would not deserve to be respected.

ALBERT CAMUS

Actuelles I, chroniques 1944–1948

What is the eternal and ultimate problem of a free society?

It is the problem of the individual who thinks that one man cannot possibly make a difference in the destiny of that society.

It is the problem of the individual who doesn't really understand the nature of a free society or what is required to make it work.

It is the problem of the individual who has no comprehension of the multiplying power of single but sovereign units.

It is the problem of the individual who regards the act of pulling a single lever in a voting booth in numerical terms rather than historical terms.

It is the problem of the individual who has no real awareness of the millions of bricks that had to be put into place, one by one, over many centuries, in order for him to dwell in the penthouse of freedom. Nor does he see any special obligation to those who continue building the structure or to those who will have to live in it after him, for better or worse.

It is the problem of the individual who recognizes no direct relationship between himself and the decisions made by government in his name. Therefore, he feels no special obligation to dig hard for the information necessary to an understanding of the issues leading to those decisions.

In short, freedom's main problem is the problem of the individual who takes himself lightly historically.

NORMAN COUSINS
Human Options

I am sad to see how many of our men and women of India who are well-bred, of high caste, of good education, and of means, who simply cannot see the truth of our cause for freedom and who simply will not involve themselves in India's problems. These good people are a curse to India— the curse of timid decency—and are a part of the tragedy of our times.

MOHANDAS GANDHI

The only thing necessary for the triumph of evil is for good [people] to do nothing.

Edmund Burke

Those who expect to reap the blessings of freedom must . . . undergo the fatigue of supporting it.

Thomas Paine

You risked your life, but what else have you ever risked? Have you ever risked disapproval? Have you ever risked economic security? Have you ever risked a belief? I see nothing particularly courageous in risking one's life. So you lose it, you go to your hero's heaven and everything is milk and honey 'til the end of time. Right? You get your reward and suffer no earthly consequences. That's not courage. Real courage is risking something you have to keep on living with, real courage is risking something that might force you to rethink your thoughts and suffer change and stretch consciousness. Real courage is risking one's clichés.

TOM ROBBINS
Another Roadside Attraction

59. Over the last two hundred years there has been a great improvement in personal and public hygiene and cleanliness; and this was largely brought about by persuading people that the results of being dirty and apathetic in the face of disease were not acts of God, but preventable acts of nature; not the sheer misery in things, but the controllable mechanisms of life.

60. We have had the first, the physical, phase of the hygienic revolution; it is time we went to the barricades for the second, the mental. Not doing good when you usefully could is not immoral; it is going about with excrement on the hands.

JOHN FOWLES

The Aristos

It is not the critic who counts, not the man who points out how the strong man stumbled, or where the doer of deeds could have done better. The credit belongs to the man who is actually in the arena, whose face is marred by dust and sweat and blood, who strives valiantly, who errs and comes short again and again, who knows the great enthusiasms, the great devotions, and spends himself in a worthy cause, who at best knows achievement and who at the worst if he fails at least fails while daring greatly so that his place shall never be with those cold and timid souls who know neither victory nor defeat.

THEODORE ROOSEVELT

(From a speech given in Paris at the Sorbonne in 1910)

(Theodore Roosevelt has been part of my consciousness since childhood. My father, like many young men of his generation, was a Teddy Roosevelt fan. He often tossed Teddy's wisdom at me, hoping it would stick and inspire. This particular quotation was passed on to me by Robert Bernstein, to whom this book is dedicated.)

I have one life and one chance to make it count for something . . . I'm free to choose what that something is, and the something I've chosen is my faith. Now, my faith goes beyond theology and religion and requires considerable work and effort. My faith demands—this is not optional—my faith *demands* that I do whatever I can, wherever I can, whenever I can, for as long as I can with whatever I have to try to make a difference.

JIMMY CARTER

(As quoted in an article in the *New York Times Magazine* written by Jim Wooten, author of *Dasher,* a biography of Jimmy Carter)

Thomas Merton wrote, "There is always a temptation to diddle around in the contemplative life, making itsy-bitsy statues." There is always an enormous temptation in all of life to diddle around making itsy-bitsy friends and meals and journeys for itsy-bitsy years on end. It is so self-conscious, so apparently moral, simply to step aside from the gaps where the creeks and winds pour down, saying, I never merited this grace, quite rightly, and then to sulk along the rest of your days on the edge of rage. I won't have it. The world is wilder than that in all directions, more dangerous and bitter, more extravagant and bright. We are making hay when we should be making whoopee; we are raising tomatoes when we should be raising Cain, or Lazarus.

ANNIE DILLARD
Pilgrim at Tinker Creek

...who will live for others shall have great troubles, but they shall seem to him small.

He who will live for himself shall have small troubles, but they shall seem to him great.

WILLIAM R. INGE

For what is a man profited, if he shall gain the whole
world, and lose his own soul? or what shall a man give
in exchange for his soul?

MATTHEW 16:26

For what shall it profit a man, if he shall gain the whole
world, and lose his own soul?

MARK 8:36

For what is a man advantaged, if he gain the whole world,
and lose himself, or be cast away?

LUKE 9:25

*(This sentiment was written right on the wall of my writing studio. It's also the
favorite quotation of my close friend Jim McDermott, an argument-loving
Irishman, who is also my representative in Congress. He insisted I had the scripture
and source wrong. We looked it up in the Bible. It's there three times in three books.
McDermott commented that God must be pretty serious about this.)*

Annotations

NORMAN COUSINS and the *Saturday Review:* The man and the influential magazine he founded and edited have not survived into this decade. And that's a great loss to the culture. His book *Human Options* includes many of his best editorial essays. He acknowledges his own debt for the character of this book to *The Practical Cogitator: The Thinker's Anthology,* published by Houghton Mifflin. This little book of classic wisdom sits alongside Cousins's on my bookshelf. Cousins dealt with his death with the same civilized and thoughtful intelligence used to edit his magazine. *Anatomy of an Illness* is a must-read for anyone who wants wise company in dealing with a terminal illness. Instead of a hospital bed and strong medication, Cousins decided to take a first-class hotel room and read nothing but humor—laughing himself back into life or laughing himself to death, whichever came first.

MOHANDAS K. GANDHI pioneered nonviolent resistance in India. He acknowledged a debt to the writings of Thoreau, especially the essay "Civil Disobedience."

EDMUND BURKE was an Irish-born English statesman, political theorist, and essayist. He is famous for his orations in the House of Commons, especially during the years of the struggles over American independence.

THOMAS PAINE, a contemporary of Burke's, was the author of some of the most provocative statements ever written regarding civil rights and religious freedom. His pamphlets *Common Sense, The Rights of Man,* and *The Age of Reason* influenced Thomas Jefferson in his public and private writings. Paine was condemned by authorities as a radical, drunken atheist and was denied burial in consecrated ground. No one knows where he was buried, but his ideas remain very much alive, embedded in law.

THEODORE ROOSEVELT was the twenty-sixth president of the United States. For all his many accomplishments and the legends built up around him, he was also a thoughtful historian. His four-volume *Winning of the West* still makes good reading. Though often thought of as a fire-eating advocate of warfare, he won the Nobel Peace Prize in 1905. He was my father's hero.

WILLIAM R. INGE was an English prelate and professor of divinity. Dean of St. Paul's, London, he was sometimes referred to as "the Gloomy Dean." Among his books were *Christian Ethics and Modern Problems* and *Our Present Discontents.*

I read TOM ROBBINS's novels with the larcenous guile of a magpie looking for shiny objects with which to decorate a nest. He's an acrobat on the highwire of language, doing astonishing feats with words and ideas. Read *Even Cowgirls Get the Blues, Jitterbug Perfume,* and *Still Life with Woodpecker.* Mind you, I don't like the plots as much as I like and underline the words, phrases, and paragraphs that stand free and sharp on their own. Robbins's asides are worth the effort of wandering around in the carnival midway of his mind.

JOHN FOWLES authored four of my favorite novels: *The Magus, The Collector, The French Lieutenant's Woman,* and *Daniel Martin.* As a literary craftsman, he has few peers. But there's more. I hold in highest esteem a small work of nonfiction, *The Aristos,* which summarizes his thinking in matters of politics, economics, art, philosophy, education, and all those fundamental matters a citizen of the world should consider. Furthermore, he revised it in later years, as he has also revised *The Magus.* His ability to consider and reconsider his craft and his life in the larger context of his existence has my deepest admiration.

Farmer, carpenter, fisherman, poet, essayist, statesman, and president are just a few of the categories for JIMMY CARTER. It is as a peacemaker that he may be best remembered in history. Like many great men, his eloquence lies more in what he *does* than what he *says.* No man stands higher in my estimation.

ANNIE DILLARD's *Pilgrim at Tinker Creek,* like Thoreau's *Walden,* is a statement about what can happen when one steps aside for a time to settle some deeply personal affairs in an environment of solitude and simplicity. I likewise treasure her *Teaching a Stone to Talk,* especially the essay, "An Expedition to the Pole." Her book of poems, *Tickets for a Prayer Wheel,* and another work of prose, *Holy the Firm,* are also on my short bookshelf of honor. Annie Dillard looks carefully at the world—looks at it straight on without blinking—and sees wide and deep. She doesn't miss a thing. As one reviewer suggests, she writes "psalms of terror and celebration."

Contra-Dictions

Fatwood is a fire starter, made when old pitchy pine tree stumps and roots are split up into finger-size kindling. A few sticks of fatwood get a fire going hot and in a hurry, even if the wood is slightly green. Once a common resource of the countryside, and usually kept neatly stacked by a kitchen stove or hearth, fatwood can now be bought in little plastic bags in city supermarkets.

I think of the quotations in this book as fatwood for my mental fire. It was a title possibility: *Fulghum's Fatwood.* But fat has unfashionably negative connotations, and most people don't burn wood, so the image is archaic. Still, there is validity in the metaphor: Fatwood comes from the heart of a tree—its flammability is derived in part from having aged well.

The quotations that follow are brief but pithy, and all have been an essential part of my fire-starting kit for a long time. All contain the flammability of timeless truth. Reliably and repeatedly, both the statements and the lives out of which they came have brought heat and light to my gloomiest ruminations. When I feel that being human is just an everlasting mix of conundrum, enigma, dilemma, paradox, illusion, and contradiction, the response I see in these quotations is, "Right—of course."

A sentence from the writing of F. Scott Fitzgerald is a case in point. In 1936 Fitzgerald published his essay "The Crack-Up" in *Esquire* magazine. Though he had, at thirty-nine, less than five more years to live, it was a swan-song description of the end game of a celebrated writer who judged himself to be a literary loser. Fitzgerald described his life as having cracked like an old plate—one that's kept around in the pantry, but no longer brought out for company. For all the early success of books like *The Great Gatsby*, for all the life of the celebrity he had lived, Fitzgerald had come to see that something was terribly wrong about the Jazz Age. The crack was not only in it, but in him. There was something he knew but could not practice— something about living with contradiction. At the outset of his essay on his breakdown, he wrote:

Before I go on with this short history, let me make a general observation—the test of a first-rate intelligence is the ability to hold two opposed ideas in the mind at the same time, and still retain the ability to function. One should, for example, be able to see that things are hopeless and yet be determined to make them otherwise.

I first found these quotes recorded in my journals in 1959. And I see that I made some alterations. My version (the alterations are underlined):

The test of being fully alive in the present world is the ability to hold two opposing ideas in the mind at the same time and still retain the ability to function.

One should be able to see that things are ultimately hopeless, and yet be determined to make them otherwise.

Happy is the man that findeth wisdom, and the man that getteth understanding.

PROVERBS 3:13

For in much wisdom is much grief: and he that increaseth knowledge increaseth sorrow.

ECCLESIASTES 1:18

(In college, I pounced upon such contradictions in the Bible as proof that the Bible was either man-made or poorly edited by God. Now I know that both statements are often true at the same time—no matter who wrote the verses.)

Do I contradict myself?
Very well then. . . . I contradict myself;
I am large. . . . I contain multitudes.

WALT WHITMAN
"Song of Myself"

(Fitzgerald made a similar observation in his notebooks: "There never was a good
biography of a good novelist. There couldn't be. He is too many people, if he's any
good.")

The man who never alters his opinion
is like standing water,
and breeds reptiles of the mind.

WILLIAM BLAKE

If you always do what you always did—
you'll always get what you always got.

UNKNOWN

(Though I've seen this statement attributed to Nick Barretta and others, I can't nail down the original source. If you know, let me know.)

There is a time in every man's education when he arrives at the conviction that envy is ignorance; that imitation is suicide; that he must take himself for better for worse as his portion . . .

It is the harder because you will always find those who think they know what is your duty better than you know it. It is easy in the world to live after the world's opinion; it is easy in solitude to live after our own; but the great man is he who in the midst of the crowd keeps with perfect sweetness the independence of solitude.

A foolish consistency is the hobgoblin of little minds . . .

RALPH WALDO EMERSON
"Self-Reliance"

For the good man to realize that it is better to be whole than to be good is to enter on a straight and narrow path compared to which his previous rectitude was flowery license.

John Middleton Murry

Early Bird

Oh, if you're a bird, be an early bird
And catch the worm for your breakfast plate.
If you're a bird, be an early early bird—
But if you're a worm, sleep late.

Shel Silverstein
Where the Sidewalk Ends

(Furthermore, if you're an early fish, you should be wary of the early worm—because he's often wrapped around a hook. A classic example of contradictory wisdom.)

There was only one catch and that was Catch-22, which specified that concern for one's own safety in the face of dangers that were real and immediate was the process of a rational mind. Orr was crazy and could be grounded. All he had to do was ask; and as soon as he did, he would no longer be crazy and would have to fly more missions. Orr would be crazy to fly more missions and sane if he didn't, but if he was sane he had to fly them. If he flew them he was crazy and didn't have to; but if he didn't want to he was sane and had to.

JOSEPH HELLER
Catch-22

There ain't no answer.
There ain't going to be any answer.
There never has been an answer.
That's the answer.

GERTRUDE STEIN

Annotations

If I published a collection of great passages from literature, notable only for their flawless beauty of expression, at least three would come from *The Great Gatsby*, by F. Scott Fitzgerald, which I keep on my read-again shelf.

Alongside it sits *The Crack-Up*, a collection of Fitzgerald's essays, letters, and notebook entries, edited by Edmund Wilson, first published in 1945 by New Directions, and still in print.

Leaves of Grass, by Walt Whitman, is unique in American literature. There's nothing quite like it—and nobody quite like him, for that matter. He said his "yes" loud and clear. You can see Whitman's thinking just beneath the surface of the poetry of Carl Sandburg.

William Blake—English poet, engraver, painter, and mystic—is as unique in English literature as Whitman is in the history of American letters. Both were trained in the making of books: Blake as an illustrator and Whitman as a printer. Both were deeply spiritual in their quest for meaning, though Blake found mystical God and Whitman found muscular Man. No single book of Blake's holds my attention, but his one-line aphorisms have a lasting power.

After reading the essays of Ralph Waldo Emerson in my freshman year of college (especially "Self-Reliance"), I wanted to know more. After reading his biography, I wanted to know more about Unitarianism. As a result, I became a Unitarian minister myself. And, in time, like him, I left the parish ministry to devote myself full-time to writing and lecturing. What is lasting about Emerson's philosophy are his brilliant epigrammatic sentences and short paragraphs summarizing long passages of exploratory thought.

JOHN MIDDLETON MURRY, literary journalist and husband of short-story writer Katherine Mansfield, was an outspoken pacifist and radical Christian mystic. In graduate school, I was affected by the thinking in his books about pacifism, William Blake, and Jesus—and by his autobiography, *Between Two Worlds*.

SHEL SILVERSTEIN is best known for his drawings and poems contained in such bestsellers as *Where the Sidewalk Ends, A Light in the Attic, The Giving Tree,* and *Falling Up.*

Although *Catch-22,* by JOSEPH HELLER, has no peer in chronicling the absurdities of World War II, Heller's novel *Something Happened* is an equally peerless account of the absurdities of the middle-class life that existed after the war. The books are not about death and horror, but about what the System does to the better inclinations of human nature. I laugh when I read Heller, fully understanding that what I'm reading isn't funny.

GERTRUDE STEIN intended her writing style to be the literary counterpart of Cubism in art. The house is divided as to whether she was a misunderstood genius or an all-too-well-understood dilettante. Still, she was at the center of a circle that included Picasso, Hemingway, Matisse, Joyce, and just about every other memorable figure in expatriate Paris before World War II. I treasure her wiggy way of nailing fragments of truth to her slightly oblique wall of wisdom.

Play

Games People Play.

Have you read that book or heard that phrase? It was also the title of a popular song. Eric Berne wrote the book and was the founding father of Transactional Analysis, the psychoanalytical theory behind the commonsense language. His theory mixed serious psychiatry with playful attitudes. I recall that the annual election of a president of the International Association of Transactional Analysis was decided by a broad-jumping contest. Playfulness mitigated the solemn business of resolving human conflict.

Berne divided the working states of the psyche into parent, adult, and child, and he helped people identify the position they took in dealing with themselves and other people. He clarified the fact that while we physically progress from child to adult, we remain capable of thinking and acting as if we were still children. There's a serious downside to this sometimes, but Berne emphasized how necessary to mental health it is to be able to be childlike one's entire life. To play, to be amused, to enjoy the moment without judgments is to have access to the child within. He insisted that this open-eyed attitude was essential for creativity, the functioning of imagination, the appreciation of beauty, the perception of art and music and poetry, and the expression of sheer joy. He insisted that allowing the child inside oneself to play is fundamental to personal sanity and a livable society. Play is not only recreation, but, in a finer sense of the word, it is a matter of creation and re-creation.

I could not agree more.

When I think of the sorrows and regrets of my life, not one of them is associated with the times I've stopped working and took time off to play.

The Fiddler of Dooney

When I play on my fiddle in Dooney,
Folk dance like a wave of the sea;
My cousin is priest in Kilvarnet,
My brother in Mocharabuiee.

I passed my brother and cousin:
They read in their books of prayer;
I read in my book of songs
I bought at the Sligo fair.

When we come at the end of time
To Peter sitting in state,
He will smile on the three old spirits,
But call me first through the gate;

For the good are always the merry,
Save by an evil chance,
And the merry love the fiddle,
And the merry love to dance:

And when the folk there spy me,
They will all come up to me,
With 'Here is the fiddler of Dooney!'
And dance like a wave of the sea.

W. B. YEATS
Collected Poems

If by eternity is understood not endless temporal duration but timelessness, then he lives eternally who lives in the present.

LUDWIG WITTGENSTEIN

Tractatus Logico-Philosophicus

Fiddler Jones

The earth keeps some vibration going
There in your heart, and that is you.
And if the people find you can fiddle,
Why, fiddle you must, for all your life.
What do you see, a harvest of clover?
Or a meadow to walk through to the river?
The wind's in the corn; you rub your hands
For beeves hereafter ready for market;
Or else you hear the rustle of skirts
Like the girls when dancing at Little Grove.
To Cooney Potter a pillar of dust
Or whirling leaves meant ruinous drouth;
They looked to me like Red-Head Sammy
Stepping it off, to "Toor-a-Loor."
How could I till my forty acres
Not to speak of getting more,
With a medley of horns, bassoons and piccolos
Stirred in my brain by crows and robins
And the creak of a wind-mill—only these?
And I never started to plow in my life
That someone did not stop in the road
And take me away to a dance or picnic.
I ended up with forty acres;
I ended up with a broken fiddle—
And a broken laugh, and a thousand memories,
And not a single regret.

EDGAR LEE MASTERS

Spoon River Anthology

. . . because we don't know [when we will die], we get to think of life as an inexhaustible well. Yet everything happens only a certain number of times, and a very small number, really. How many more times will you remember a certain afternoon of your childhood, some afternoon that's so deeply a part of your being that you can't even conceive of your life without it? Perhaps four or five times more. Perhaps not even that. How many more times will you watch the full moon rise? Perhaps twenty. And yet it all seems limitless.

PAUL BOWLES
The Sheltering Sky

(An adaptation of these words is carved on the tombstone of Brandon Lee, son of the legendary martial arts master Bruce Lee. Father and son are buried side-by-side, both having died tragic deaths at a young age. Their graves are about ten yards from my own cemetery plot. When I walk by my grave site from time to time, I always pass by and read these words. I usually go away with my attitude about life clarified.)

You can understand and relate to most people better if you look at them—no matter how old or impressive they may be—as if they are children. For most of us never really grow up or mature all that much—we simply grow taller. Oh, to be sure, we laugh less and play less and wear uncomfortable disguises like adults, but beneath the costume is the child we always are, whose needs are simple, whose daily life is still best described by fairy tales.

LEO ROSTEN

Each fairy tale is a magic mirror which reflects some aspects of our inner world, and of the steps required by our evolution from immaturity to maturity. For those who immerse themselves in what the fairy tale has to communicate, it becomes a deep, quiet pool which at first seems to reflect only our own image; but behind it we soon discover the inner turmoils of our soul—its depth, and ways to gain peace within ourselves and with the world, which is the reward of our struggles.

Bruno Bettelheim

The Uses of Enchantment

Each of the classic fairy tales has been honed and polished and perfected by the minds and spirits and needs and wisdom of millions of people across hundreds, perhaps thousands, of years. The richness of the human journey is here. Listen. Pass it on. So that there will not pass from our future the enchantment that begins with the honored words, "Once upon a time, long ago and far away, in a deep forest, there lived a child—much like you."

(In an old journal, I found these two paragraphs. The first is Bettelheim's; the second may or may not be. But I include it here because of its truth.)

Ever since there have been men, man has given himself over to too little joy. That alone, my brothers, is our original sin. I should believe only in a God who understood how to dance.

HENRI MATISSE

What is precious is never to forget
The essential delight of the blood drawn from ageless
    springs
Breaking through rocks in worlds before our earth.
Never to deny its pleasure in the morning simple light
Nor its grave evening demand for love.
Never to allow gradually the traffic to smother
With noise and fog, the flowering of the Spirit.

STEPHEN SPENDER

"I Think Continually of Those Who Were Truly Great"

The Balinese have much to teach us about the (non) art of celebration. The making of splendid occasions occupies much of their time. If you ask a Balinese what he does, he will proudly answer, "I am a Baris dancer" or "I am a mask maker." If you persist and ask again, "No, I mean how do you get your rice?" he loses interest, his voice drops, he may turn away, deciding this is a pretty boring conversation. "Oh that," he will say.

CORITA KENT

It is difficult
to get the news from poems
yet men die miserably every day
for lack
of what is found there.

WILLIAM CARLOS WILLIAMS
"Asphodel, That Greeny Flower,"
from *Pictures from Brueghel and Other Poems*

(Williams has been an important influence on my life not only because of his powerful poetry, but because he managed to carry on a successful career as a pediatrician while writing poetry, novels, and plays. His combination of professions helped justify my own mixture of parallel careers.)

How Can I Keep from Singing

My life flows on in endless song,
Above earth's lamentations
I hear the real tho' far off hymn,
That hails a new creation.

Thru all the tumult and the strife,
I hear that music ringing,
It sounds an echo in my soul,
How can I keep from singing?
What tho' the tempest round me roars,
I know the truth it liveth,
What tho' the darkness round me close
Songs in the night it giveth,
No storm can shake my inmost calm,
While to that rock I'm clinging—
Since love is lord of heaven and earth
How can I keep from singing?

ANNE WARNER
(Arranged and performed by Pete Seeger)

One of the temptations of the artist is to believe himself solitary, and in truth he hears this shouted at him with a certain base delight. But this is not true. He stands in the midst of all, in the same rank, neither higher nor lower, with all those who are working and struggling. His very vocation, in the face of oppression, is to open the prisons and to give a voice to the sorrows and joys of all. This is where art, against its enemies, justifies itself by proving precisely that it is no one's enemy. By itself art could probably not produce the renascence which implies justice and liberty. But without it, that renascence would be without forms and, consequently, would be nothing. Without culture, and the relative freedom it implies, society, even when perfect, is but a jungle. This is why any authentic creation is a gift to the future.

ALBERT CAMUS
"The Myth of Sisyphus"

There are at least two kinds of games. One could be called finite, the other infinite.

A finite game is played for the purpose of winning, an infinite game for the purpose of continuing the play.

Finite players play within boundaries; infinite players play with boundaries.

Surprise causes finite play to end; it is the reason for infinite play to continue.

To be prepared against surprise is to be trained. To be prepared for surprise is to be educated.

The finite play for life is serious; the infinite play of life is joyous.

The joyfulness of infinite play, its laughter, lies in learning to start something we cannot finish.

No one can play a game alone. One cannot be human by oneself.

Our social existence has . . . an inescapably fluid character.

. . . we are not the stones over which the stream of the world flows; we are the stream itself.

Change itself is the very basis of our continuity as persons.

y that which can change can continue: this is the prin-
le by which infinite players live.

JAMES P. CARSE
Finite and Infinite Games

(These are sentences I chose to summarize a line of thinking from a small book that affected my thinking in a big way. See the annotations section for more about Carse.)

Lee-la, Lee-la, this life is but a game.
Winners lose and losers win, the game is still the same.
Lee-la, Lee-la, this life is but a play.
Those who say they know, don't know.
And those who know, don't say.

BILLY SCHWARTZ

(Sung to a Nepalese fiddle tune)

(I include this with some trepidation over its source, but not its meaning. I've had it in my keepsake file for a long time, but I have seen several versions of it, credited to several authors. Its roots are very old—deep in the Tantric traditions of India.)

Annotations

WILLIAM BUTLER YEATS—Irish poet, essayist, novelist, and playwright—won the Nobel Prize in Literature in 1923. When he prepared his *Collected Poems,* he rewrote many of them. Yeats is one of my favorite poets.

LUDWIG WITTGENSTEIN's life is as interesting as his philosophy was influential. Coming from a famous Viennese family, he was not only a professor at Cambridge University and a close associate of Bertrand Russell's, but he retreated from academia to teach primary school in Austria. His thinking was essential to the development of logical positivism and an attempt to say things clearly and simply. He felt that modern philosophy "is a battle against the bewitchment of our intelligence by means of language." His biography makes fascinating reading.

Spoon River Anthology, by EDGAR LEE MASTERS, contains not only some words I wish I wrote—I wish I had written the whole thing. It's a unique and powerful literary masterpiece—part history, part poetry, part sociology—giving voice to the people buried in the cemetery of a small midwestern town, expressing the truths that only the dead can know.

PAUL BOWLES has lived in Morocco for the past forty years. *The Sheltering Sky* was his first and finest novel—very much in the vein of Lawrence Durrell's Alexandria Quartet. He is also a composer of classical music and film scores. His autobiography, *Without Stopping,* is worth reading if you are interested in the life of an expatriate artist.

While HENRI MATISSE needs no introduction as an artist, what he had to say about his art is less well known. My thinking about my own painting was influenced by contact with the American master Richard Diebenkorn, and he, in turn, was much influenced by Matisse.

STEPHEN SPENDER was an English poet, essayist, literary critic, and social activist. He wrote a thoughtful autobiography entitled *World Within World*.

CORITA KENT was a Roman Catholic nun—a member of the Immaculate Heart community in Los Angeles. She was an inspiration as an artist and teacher of art, able to find meaning in common things and to inspire the least talented high school student to make art.

WILLIAM CARLOS WILLIAMS lived out most of his adult life in Rutherford, New Jersey, practicing medicine by day and writing poetry by night. As a small-town physician, he often saw humanity at its best and worst. As a poet, he found reason to exalt what he saw in such a way that he affected the shape of modern American poetry. He called his approach "objectivism."

PETE SEEGER: folksinger, songwriter, essayist, and social activist for human rights, peace, free speech, and integration. He sang with Woody Guthrie, the Weavers, and just about every other important folk musician of the twentieth century. In my pantheon of heroes, he sits in the first rank, banjo in hand.

With an expansive sense of humor and a scholar's love of language, LEO ROSTEN has made his life and living out of being Jewish. He's written novels, short stories, film scripts, essays, and many works of nonfiction. I use, enjoy, and recommend his *Joys of Yiddish; Infinite Riches: Gems from a Lifetime of Reading; The Power of Positive Nonsense; Rome*

Wasn't Burned in a Day: The Mischief of Language; and *A New Guide and Almanac to the Religions of America.* I buy anything he writes or edits, knowing I will learn something useful, will have some good laughs, and will have been in fine company. He's on my list of people I wish I lived next door to.

Bruno Bettelheim studied psychotherapy with Freud in Vienna. During the Nazi regime, he was imprisoned at Dachau and Buchenwald. His two books on his concentration camp experiences are unforgettable: *The Informed Heart* and *Surviving the Holocaust.* Of all his books on psychotherapy, none more influenced my thinking than his writing about the power of fairy tales in *The Uses of Enchantment.*

James P. Carse is a professor of religion at New York University and a winner of that university's Great Teacher Award. One aspect of being a great teacher is to get a student to consider the obvious in such a new light that not only is his or her thinking changed, but the process of how to think is itself affected. Such was my experience in reading *Finite and Infinite Games.* Unable to find it in hardcover, I had a paperback copy more permanently bound in bright red leather. It sits alongside my copy of Thoreau's *Walden,* which indicates its importance in the development of both my thinking and my thinking about thinking. It was published by The Free Press, a division of Macmillan, in 1986.

Companions

"He would walk into my mind as if it were a town and he a torchlight procession of one, lighting up the streets . . ."

Words of a graveside eulogy of one friend for another, as related by Nobel Prize–winning poet Seamus Heaney in his book *The Redress of Poetry.*

"Where's home for you?" a stranger asks a fellow traveler on a plane.

"Wherever she is," comes the reply, as the man points at his wife.

"They're a two-man party in a movable tavern where it's never closing time," says a woman of her husband and his lifelong buddy sitting offshore in a small rowboat, laughing and talking and semi-fishing.

"The kinship of blood is forever, but it is not a choice; marriage is a choice, but it is held together by laws and kids and habits; but friendship—heart-to-heart and man-to-man friendship—is stronger than blood and longer than love. I would rather have an old friend than an old brother or an old wife." So says a Greek barber.

"You're judged by the company you keep," said my father.

"Your father hangs out with jackasses and drunks," said my mother.

"He was his own best friend—always alone, but never

lonely," said a sad widow of her dead ex-husband at his memorial service. "But I always thought when he was alone he was in bad company."

Conversation overheard at a bus stop:
"Did Jesus ever have a friend? Oh, sure, he had followers and disciples, but did he have a real buddy? No."
"But it's always lonely at the top."
"Yeah, but it's lonely at the bottom, too, and at the bottom you at least got company."

And so on. Very few of us can go all the way alone. Everybody needs somebody sometime.

"What is REAL?" asked the Rabbit one day, when they were lying side by side. . . . "Does it mean having things that buzz inside you and a stick-out-handle?"

"Real isn't how you are made," said the Skin Horse. "It's a thing that happens to you. When a child loves you for a long, long time, not just to play with, but REALLY loves you, then you become Real."

"Does it hurt?" asked the Rabbit.

"Sometimes," said the Skin Horse, for he was always truthful. "When you are Real you don't mind being hurt."

"Does it happen all at once, like being wound up," he asked, "or bit by bit?"

"It doesn't happen all at once," said the Skin Horse. "You become. It takes a long time. That's why it doesn't often happen to people who break easily, or have sharp edges, or who have to be carefully kept. Generally, by the time you are Real, most of your hair has been loved off, and your eyes drop out and you get loose in the joints and very shabby. But these things don't matter at all, because once you are Real you can't be ugly, except to people who don't understand."

MARGERY WILLIAMS
The Velveteen Rabbit

The second principle of magic: . . . things which have once been in contact with each other continue to act on each other at a distance after the physical contact has been severed.

SIR JAMES G. FRAZER
The Golden Bough

You that would judge me do not judge alone
This book or that, come to this hallowed place
Where my friends' portraits hang and look thereon;
Ireland's history in their lineaments trace;
Think where man's glory most begins and ends
And say my glory was I had such friends.

W. B. YEATS
"The Municipal Gallery Re-visited" in *The Collected Poems*

The Spider's Web (Natural History)

The spider dropping down from twig
Unfolds a plan of her devising
A thin premeditated rig
To use in rising.

And all that journey down from space,
In cool descent and loyal hearted
She spins a ladder to the place
From where she started.

Thus I, gone forth as spiders do
In spider's web a truth discerning,
Attach one silken strand to you
For my returning.

E. B. White

Although I conquer all the earth,
yet for me there is only one city.
In that city there is for me only one house;
And in that house, one room only;
And in that room, a bed.
And one woman sleeps there,
The shining joy and jewel of all my kingdom.

SANSKRIT POEM
(Translated by John Brough)

There are those who really never know their minds.
They're confused and they're not the stayin' kind.
They don't know what they're really lookin' for.
I don't suffer from that problem anymore.

Chorus:
You could send me away and I would go.
I would go but I would not go too far.
You could send me home but you would know,
Home to me is anywhere you are.

TOM PAXTON
"Home to Me"

It's no good trying to fool yourself about love. You can't fall into it like a soft job, without dirtying up your hands. It takes muscle and guts. And if you can't bear the thought of messing up your nice, clean soul, you'd better give up the whole idea of life, and become a saint. Because you'll never make it as a human being. It's either this world or the next.

JOHN OSBORNE

(Jimmy speaking to Helena, in the play
Look Back in Anger)

If you're down and confused
And you don't remember who you're talkin' to
Concentration slip away
'Cause your baby is so far away
Well, there's a rose in the fisted glove
And the eagle flies with the dove.
And if you can't be with the one you love,
Love the one you're with
Love the one you're with.

STEPHEN STILLS

"Love the One You're With"

(If you don't know this song, you weren't alert or alive in the sixties. I've paraphrased the theme many times as an admonition to cynics: If you can't have the world you want, honey, love the world you have.)

For nothing is fixed, forever and forever and forever,
is not fixed; the earth is always shifting, the light is
always changing, the sea does not cease to grind down
rock. Generations do not cease to be born, and we are
responsible to them because we are the only witnesses
they have. The sea rises, the light fails, lovers cling to each
other, and children cling to us. The moment we cease to
hold each other, the moment we break faith with one
another, the sea engulfs us and the light goes out.

JAMES BALDWIN
Nothing Personal

. . . in the small matters trust the mind,
in the large ones the heart. . . .

SIGMUND FREUD

And now here is my secret, a very simple secret:
It is only with the heart that one can see rightly;
what is essential is invisible to the eye.

ANTOINE DE SAINT-EXUPÉRY
The Little Prince

Annotations

MARGERY WILLIAMS wrote many books for adults under the name of Margery Bianco. *The Velveteen Rabbit; or How Toys Become Real* belongs alongside *The Little Prince* in the unique class of children's stories that speak just as meaningfully to adults.

The Golden Bough, a twelve-volume work published in 1915 by SIR JAMES GEORGE FRAZER, a Scottish anthropologist, is the essential reference for anyone interested in the origins of cults and myths and magic as applied to the development of religion.

E. B. WHITE wrote a great many things I wish I wrote: *Charlotte's Web,* the best children's/adult novel ever; *The Second Tree from the Corner,* which contains my favorite short essay by the same title; the edited revision of William Strunk's *The Elements of Style,* the best set of rules and advice for the writer; and about fifty short pieces for *The New Yorker* magazine that cannot be improved upon for clarity, humor, and wisdom. His collected letters, essays, poems, and biography are all worth reading. He was ill-labeled a humorist. He was a deep and serious man who used a sense of humor as a sauce for substantial fare.

It would be insufficient to call TOM PAXTON a folksinger. It's a category too often meant to diminish. All music is folk music—made by folks, not animals or machines. Paxton is a brilliant poet, acerbic political commentator, and thoughtful philosopher who has for decades used words and lyrics as well as humor to critically celebrate the life he sees and lives. I have all his albums, listen to them regularly, and know many of his songs by heart. Four favorite albums:

And Loving You, *It Ain't Easy*, *Politics Live* (released by Flying Fish Records), and *Live for the Record* (on the Sugar Hill label).

JOHN OSBORNE, an English playwright at the center of a generation of antiestablishment writers known as the Angry Young Men. *Look Back in Anger* was his first and most famous of many works for the theater.

ANTOINE DE SAINT-EXUPÉRY—French novelist, essayist, and pioneering aviator—is best known for *Le Petit Prince,* or *The Little Prince,* whose power comes from its being a fine children's fairy tale with lasting meaning for adults. He and his little prince are featured on the new French fifty-franc banknote. His barely fictionalized personal experiences as an aviator became fine novels. My favorites are *Night Flight* and *Wind, Sand, and Stars. Flight to Arras* is an autobiographical account of a dangerous wartime mission as exciting as anything in fiction. He disappeared on a flight over occupied France in 1944.

Lafter

(YELLOW LIGHT. CAUTION. Take your time with this next paragraph. It's full of potholes, and it's easier if you read it aloud and stay mentally loose.)

Win eye wuz uh teechur—uh ort teechur—eye rote ass-ein-mints 2 d stewed-ants n d class you-sink lang-which lak dis. It waz uh weigh off kip-ink uh lite-horted n luce attic-tyoud bout sear-he-us wirk. D stewed-ants thot et wuz fun-he. D Angwish tee-churs dead-knot. Dey sed eye wuz may-kink stew-pid trubbull. Eye all-weighs re-furred dim 2 d holy right-ink uf d fey-moose rite-her Chames Choice, two ream-ind dim dat lang-witch s a kind off play. N leyef s a kind off choke. Lafter n lern-ink n he-maj-he-nay-shun r ee-sin-shall 2 cree-ate-hiv-itty, witch s ee-sin-shall 2 sieve-ee-lie-za-shun. Oh, Kay?

Now, ewe no y dis chapped-her hed-ink s speld rong. C? Lafter.

10 Q fairy mush 4 yur pay-shuns, n gud luk.

Recently, I was trapped in a lecture hall while a respectable scholar delivered a lengthy *monologue* on the value of *dialogue* in human affairs. Faking hiccups to suppress cackles of dismay, I just made it out of the room before losing control of my urge to laugh. It reminded me of a similarly *wordy* lecture I heard extolling the virtues of *silence.* Not everybody thought these ironic presentations funny, which is part of the squirrelly nature of laughter.

In light of such memories, I hesitate to write much about lafter. I'd rather show you the best cartoons of Gary Larson from *The Far Side,* play you a recording of Woody Allen doing his best stand-up comedy routines, read you a Dave Barry column or two, and sing you some choices from the Monty Python songbook. Then you'd know what makes me laugh and why. And if you laughed as well, we wouldn't need to have a discussion about the meaning and importance of laughter.

Nothing connects me with a person quicker than knowing what he laughs at. Nothing is more valuable in a relationship than loose and easy laughter.

I know no wiser words than the stainless steel truth that he who laughs, lasts.

There is a species of primate in South America, more gregarious than most other mammals, with a curious behavior. The members of this species often gather in groups, large and small, and in the course of their mutual chattering, under a wide variety of circumstances, they are induced to engage in bouts of involuntary, convulsive respiration, a sort of loud, helpless, mutually reinforcing group panting that sometimes is so severe as to incapacitate them. Far from being aversive, however, these attacks seem to be sought out by most members of the species, some of whom appear to be addicted to them.

We might be tempted to think that if only we knew what it was like to be them, from the inside, we'd understand this curious addiction of theirs. If we could see it "from their point of view," we would know what it was for. But in this case we can be quite sure that such insight as we might gain would still leave matters mysterious. For we already have the access we seek; the species is *Homo sapiens* (which does indeed inhabit South America, among other places), and the behavior is laughter.

Daniel C. Dennett

Consciousness Explained

For the reason of laughter, since laughter is surely
The surest touch of genius in creation.
Would you ever have thought of it, I ask you,
If you had been making man, stuffing him full
Of such hopping greeds and passions that he has
To blow himself to pieces as often as he
Conveniently can manage it—would it also
Have occurred to you to make him burst himself
With such a phenomenon as cachinnation?
That same laughter, madam, is an irrelevancy
Which almost amounts to revelation.

CHRISTOPHER FRY
The Lady's Not for Burning

All things dull and ugly
All creatures short and squat
All things rude and nasty
The Lord God made the lot

Each little snake that poisons
Each little wasp that stings
He made their brutish venom
He made their horrid wings

All things sick and cancerous
All evil great and small
All things foul and dangerous
The Lord God made them all

Each nasty little hornet
Each beastly little squid
Who made the spikey urchin?
Who made the sharks? He did.

All things scabbed and ulcerous
All pox both great and small
Putrid foul and gangrenous,
The Lord God made them all
AMEN

ERIC IDLE

Once upon a time there were four little Rabbits, and their names were—Flopsy, Mopsy, Cotton-tail, and Peter. They lived with their Mother in a sand-bank, underneath the root of a very big fir-tree.

"Now, my dears," said old Mrs. Rabbit one morning, "you may go into the fields or down the lane, but don't go into Mr. McGregor's garden: your Father had an accident there, he was put in a pie by Mrs. McGregor."

BEATRIX POTTER
The Tale of Peter Rabbit

(This touch of macabre realism is in what is often thought of as a sweet children's story. My mother and I always laughed at the thought of the father bunny being killed and cooked and eaten. I wonder if Ms. Potter considered the oedipal implications?)

When I die, I want to go peacefully and quietly in
my sleep like my grandfather did—not screaming and
shouting like the passengers in his car at the time.

UNKNOWN

The Least Successful Animal Rescue

The firemen's strike of 1978 made possible one of the great animal rescue attempts of all time. Valiantly, the British Army had taken over emergency firefighting and on 14 January they were called out by an elderly lady in South London to retrieve her cat which had become trapped up a tree. They arrived with impressive haste and soon discharged their duty. So grateful was the lady that she invited them all in for tea. Driving off later, with fond farewells completed, they ran over the cat and killed it.

The Vet Who Surprised a Cow

In the course of his duties in August 1977, a Dutch veterinary surgeon was required to treat an ailing cow. To investigate its internal gases he inserted a tube into that end of the animal not capable of facial expression and struck a match. The jet of flame set fire first to some bales of hay and then to the whole farm causing damage estimated at £45,000. The vet was later fined £140 for starting a fire in a manner surprising to the magistrates. The cow escaped with shock.

STEPHEN PILE
The Incomplete Book of Failures

LOSER SEEKS MATE: Lazy, spoiled, insensitive, irresponsible, insecure, desperate SWM. Hate art, travel, reading, and exercise. Like tuna noodle casserole, miniature golf, and tattoos. Love sitting, sleeping, drinking beer, and watching nature films on TV. YOU, a SWF, former cheerleader with amnesia, earn 100K from a trust fund and would enjoy romantic evenings doing my laundry and cleaning my house. Sex is optional—only when I opt. Saving grace—a great sense of humor.

PERSONAL AD IN A WEEKLY NEWSPAPER

Murphy's Laws

If anything can go wrong, it will.
If anything can't go wrong, it still will.
Nothing is ever as simple as it seems.
Everything takes longer than you expect.
Whatever you set out to do, something else must be
    done first.
You can't do just one thing—there are always consequences.
If everything seems to be going well, you have obviously
    overlooked something.
Nature always sides with the hidden flaw.
Mother Nature is a bitch.
It's impossible to make anything foolproof, because fools
    are so ingenious.
Always lie low—you can't fall off the floor.
Never lose heart—they might want to cut it out.
You can fool some of the people all of the time and all of
    the people some of the time, and that's sufficient.

*(Murphy's Laws are ubiquitous, but the most serious collector and publisher of them
is Paul Dickson.)*

Pain is deeper than all thought,
laughter is higher than all pain.

ELBERT HUBBARD

Annotations

DANIEL C. DENNETT is an Oxford-educated philosopher. His book *Consciousness Explained*, published in 1991, is already a classic in cross-referential thinking, mixing philosophy, psychology, physiology, and social sciences into a fresh view of the human mind.

CHRISTOPHER FRY, English dramatist, is noted for writing comedies with serious undertones. In addition to *The Lady's Not for Burning*, I recommend his religious play, *A Sleep of Prisoners*, as well as his autobiography, *Can You Find Me: A Family History*.

ERIC IDLE, of Monty Python, wrote the lyrics for the song "All Things Dull and Ugly."

The Tale of Peter Rabbit began as a letter to a sick child and was first published privately in 1900 by its author and illustrator, BEATRIX POTTER. She went on to produce twenty-three stories, combining charming fictional characters with stories of honest realism. My other favorite is *The Tale of Jemima Puddle-Duck*, who, in any time of crisis, would say, "Let us find a convenient dry nesting place."

PAUL DICKSON, like Leo Rosten, is a man in love with language and humor. *The Official Rules; The Official Explanations; Toasts; Words; Names; The Mature Person's Guide to Kites, Yo-yos, Frisbees, and Other Childlike Diversions;* and *There Are Alligators in the Sewers and Other American Credos* are the titles of just a few of Dickson's productions that I've enjoyed and used and kept.

Believe

Here's something I wrote in 1965. Shared without revision. Most of what I've found in my files from more than thirty years ago has merit only as biographical footnotes about the road I was headed down at the time. But this little essay is not all that shabby. And the belief it expresses has not changed. In fact, I hold it with even more conviction now. The essay is entitled "Parades and Circuses." I don't know quite why.

Met a man today. Man I had seen many times before. Just sitting. With his legs crossed, hands knotted together, head hanging, hat down, and collar up. A daily fixture on the stone bench across from the children's fountain on the town green. Asleep, I think. But his lips are moving—very carefully moving. An ordinary average-middle kind of man. Size, age, clothes, condition—all ordinary average-middle. From one to two each day he sat—undisturbed by dogs, children, buses, laughter, rain, or cold. He sat. Saying something to himself, maybe. Daily.

So I asked him. One day I had to ask him. Asked him was he all right (which meant, "what's going on, buddy?").

And you know what he said? Said he was praying. Praying. Not that praying is so strange, but he said he was praying the alphabet. Just reciting the alphabet over and over for an hour each day, leaving it to Almighty God to arrange the letters into the proper words of a proper prayer. What was missing in words, he said, he made up for in fervor. He figured God could handle it and would understand.

Well. I don't know. I think maybe I would settle for a little

less praying and a little more sanity, myself. At the same time.
At the same time, I wish I believed in something—had faith in
something—that much.

Faith is a determination to keep in touch with the
unnameable Being that dwells in the heart of all existence—
you and me, included. Whatever works to accomplish that
is valid. I actually have a homemade prayer string now, with
beads and amulets and stones and talismans and bones rep-
resenting many faiths and many religious experiences. All
the letters of the alphabet are there—the Greek alphabet,
actually, to emphasize the mystery of language itself. In
quiet moments alone I say my beads—I use the items strung
together as a memory device, serving the same purpose for
me as rereading the quotations in this book.

This is what I believe:

That I am I.
That my soul is a dark forest.
That my known self will never be more than a little
     clearing in the forest.
That gods, strange gods, come forth from the forest into
     the clearing of my known self, and then go back.
That I must have the courage to let them come and go.
That I will never let mankind put anything over me, but
     that I will try always to recognize and submit to the
     gods in me and the gods in other men and women.

There is my creed.

D. H. LAWRENCE
Studies in Classic American Literature

ANNIE: I believe in the Church of Baseball. I tried all the major religions and most of the minor ones. I've worshipped Buddha, Allah, Brahma, Vishnu, Siva, trees, mushrooms and Isadora Duncan. I know things. For instance: there are 108 beads in a Catholic rosary and there are 108 stitches in a baseball. When I learned that, I gave Jesus a chance. But it just didn't work out between us. The Lord laid out too much guilt on me. I prefer metaphysics to theology. You see, there's no guilt in baseball and it's never boring, which makes it like sex.

CRASH: Well, I believe in the soul, the cock, the pussy, the small of a woman's back, the hangin' curveball, high fiber, good scotch, that the novels of Susan Sontag are self-indulgent, overrated crap. . . . I believe in the sweet spot, soft-core pornography, opening your presents Christmas morning rather than Christmas Eve, and I believe in long, slow, deep, soft, wet kisses that last three days.

ANNIE: Oh my.

RON SHELTON
(*Dialogue from the movie* Bull Durham)

—Look here, Cranly, he said. You have asked me what
I would do and what I would not do. I will tell you what
I will do and what I will not do. I will not serve that in
which I no longer believe, whether it call itself my home,
my fatherland, or my church: and I will try to express
myself in some mode of life or art as freely as I can and as
wholly as I can, using for my defence the only arms I allow
myself to use—silence, exile, and cunning. . . .

—You made me confess the fears that I have. But I will
tell you also what I do not fear. I do not fear to be alone
or to be spurned for another or to leave whatever I have to
leave. And I am not afraid to make a mistake, even a great
mistake, a lifelong mistake, and perhaps as long as eternity
too.

JAMES JOYCE
A Portrait of the Artist as a Young Man

the lesson of the moth

i was talking to a moth
the other evening
he was trying to break into
an electric light bulb
and fry himself on the wires

why do you fellows
pull this stunt I asked him
because it is the conventional
thing for moths or why
if that had been an uncovered
candle instead of an electric
light bulb you would
now be a small unsightly cinder
have you no sense

plenty of it he answered
but at times we get tired
of using it
we get bored with the routine
and crave beauty
and excitement
fire is beautiful
and we know that if we get
too close it will kill us
but what does that matter
it is better to be happy
for a moment

and be burned up with beauty
than to live a long time
and be bored all the while
so we wad all our life up
into one little roll
and then we shoot the roll
that is what life is for
it is better to be a part of beauty
for one instant and then cease to
exist than to exist forever
and never be a part of beauty
our attitude toward life
is come easy go easy
we are like human beings
used to be before they became
too civilized to enjoy themselves

and before I could argue him
out of his philosophy
he went and immolated himself
on a patent cigar lighter
I do not agree with him
myself I would rather have
half the happiness and twice
the longevity

but at the same time I wish
there was something I wanted
as badly as he wanted to fry himself
                                    archy

DON MARQUIS
Archy and Mehitabel

You must always be intoxicated.

That sums it all up: it's the only question. In order not to feel the horrible burden of Time which breaks your back and bends you down to earth, you must be unremittingly intoxicated.

But on what? Wine, poetry, virtue, as you please. But never be sober.

And if it should chance that sometimes, on the steps of a palace, on the green grass of a ditch, in the bleak solitude of your room, you wake up and your intoxication has already diminished or disappeared, ask the wind, the wave, the star, the bird, the clock, ask everything that flees, everything that groans, everything that rolls, everything that sings, everything that speaks, ask them what time it is and the wind, the wave, the star, the bird, the clock, will reply: It's time to be intoxicated!

If you do not wish to be one of the tortured slaves of Time, never be sober; never ever be sober! Use wine, poetry, or virtue, as you please.

CHARLES-PIERRE BAUDELAIRE
The Prose Poems and La Fanfarlo

People are defeated or go mad or die in many, many ways, some in the silence of that valley, *where I couldn't hear nobody pray* and many in the public, sounding horror where no cry or lament or song or hope can disentangle itself from the roar. And so we go under, victims of that universal cruelty which lives in the heart and in the world, victims of the universal indifference to the fate of another, victims of the universal fear of love, proof of the absolute impossibility of achieving a life without love. One day, perhaps, unimaginable generations hence, we will evolve into the knowledge that human beings are more important than real estate and will permit this knowledge to become the ruling principle of our lives. For I do not for an instant doubt, and I will go to my grave believing that we can build Jerusalem, if we will.

JAMES BALDWIN
Nothing Personal

Sometimes it rains on the just. I believe that.
Sometimes it rains on the unjust. I believe that, too.
But I also believe that sometimes it just rains.
Neither God or Justice or belief has anything to do with it.

Anonymous

Annotations

D. H. LAWRENCE is best known for *Lady Chatterley's Lover,* which still makes good reading, though it's hard to believe it was banned as pornographic. His statement about belief comes in response to what he perceived to be the cloying values of Benjamin Franklin. He was wrong about Franklin.

The talented RON SHELTON got his B.A. in English, played minor league baseball for five years, got an M.F.A. in sculpture, and then turned to writing film scripts. His credits include one of my all-time favorite movies, the award-winning *Bull Durham.* He also wrote *Blaze, White Men Can't Jump, Cobb,* and *Tin Cup.*

Any modern writer in the English language owes a great debt to JAMES JOYCE and can take from him a lifelong lesson in the craft. I read and reread *Finnegans Wake* for its wordplay and ideaplay as much as anything else. Joyce's book *Dubliners* contains "The Dead," one of the best short stories ever written.

DON MARQUIS was an American newspaperman and humorist who wrote for the *New York Sun* and the *New York Herald Tribune.* Archy was a literary cockroach who typed one letter at a time by landing on the keys—no capital letters—and Mehitabel was a cat who served as a foil for Archy's commentary on human behavior. The essays and poems were collected in a volume named after the two characters.

CHARLES-PIERRE BAUDELAIRE—essayist, translator, critic, and poet—gained fame with his small book of sensual poems, *Les Fleurs du Mal,* for which he was prosecuted for obscenity and blasphemy. The content seems tame by present criteria, but the affirmation of sensual beauty remains a standard by which modern French poetry is still judged.

God

In the credo I wrote at age twenty-one, the longest part was devoted to God.

It was a Supreme Court appeal against the existence of the Sunday-school version of the deity imposed on me in childhood. On reading my fiercely argued case, one professor said that not only had I thrown the baby out with the bathwater, but I had thrown out the soap and towel and bathtub as well—and then tried to burn down the bathroom while I was at it. Destruction without construction. Was there nothing, he asked, that might replace what I had so thoroughly rejected? At the time, the answer was NO, absolutely not.

Now, in this present credo pentimento, I see many layers of paint applied over that NO. Visible are faint remnants of a design for an accommodation with the idea of God as I have struggled for a self-portrait of my soul. I could construct an existential road map marking the long distances traveled and the varied destinations visited in search of a reconciliation with an unrelenting yearning to settle something in my mind once and for all.

And it is settled.

(Having written that, I smile. I've thought that before, only to find myself back on the pilgrim's road in the company of angels and demons once again.) What I *should* say is that the God issue is settled *for now.* Settled like the phases of the moon are settled. By that I mean I understand my perception of the variable pattern of the moon's activity. The moon apparently comes, apparently changes appearance, and apparently goes, only to come again. But its apparent nature depends largely on my point of view. I would think of it differently if I saw it from Mars.

Same thing for the matter of death. It comes. Reliably. You can count on it. But you can see it from only the point of view of being alive.

I would not evangelize door-to-door about the moon or death. My interest in further discussion of the things I'm clear on is slight. The obvious doesn't need a defense attorney.

Recently, I was an accidental guest at an international gathering of theologians held near where I live in Greece. When the learned professors began shaving at each other's thinking about God with the finely honed razors of their intellects, I quietly escaped the room. The debate didn't engage me. Walking away into the morning quietness of the nearby hills covered with olive trees satisfied my spiritual needs far more than the verbal gymnastics of the theologians.

So, then, you might ask, where *do* I stand? Can I provide the working definition of the nature of God as I express it now? No. And I decline to try. Not because I'm unsure of my position. To the contrary. I realize that what has separated me from God is not doubt but beliefs and creeds and formulas. My feelings and thoughts have passed over into that place where words cannot go—into namelessness. Beyond theology, scripture, and church. And beyond expression. I cannot take you there. Nor would I insist you go my way—or even go at all. It's a hard trip, through brambles and over barren ground, in storm and darkness. I only say you may go if you must. And you may take heart in knowing others have gone before you.

I thought through this essay while sitting on a bench in a

cemetery, near my own grave site. It's a place of perspective I visit from time to time. As I stood up to walk home, some words written by the poet Rainer Maria Rilke came to mind—as good a summary statement about God as I know. Words I wish I wrote:

I live my life in growing orbits which move out over this wondrous world. I am circling around God, around the ancient towers and I have been circling for a thousand years. And I still don't know if I am an eagle or a storm or a great song.

We have seen the highest circle of spiraling powers.

We have named this circle God. We might have given it any name we wished: Abyss, Absolute Darkness, Absolute Light, Matter, Spirit, Ultimate Hope, Ultimate Despair, Silence. But never forget, it is we who give it a name.

NIKOS KAZANTZAKIS

Human speech is like a cracked kettle on which we tap crude rhythms for bears to dance to, while we long to make music that will melt the stars.

GUSTAVE FLAUBERT
Madame Bovary

The kingdom of God is within you.

LUKE 17:21

The eye with which I see God
Is the very same eye with which God sees me.

MEISTER ECKHART

The world stands out on either side—
No wider than the heart is wide;
Above the world is stretched the sky,
No higher than the soul is high.

Edna St. Vincent Millay
"Renascence"

For God to me, it seems
is a verb
not a noun,
proper or improper;
is the articulation
not the art . . .
is loving,
not the abstraction of love . . .

Yes, God is a verb,
the most active, connoting the vast harmonic
reordering of the universe
from the unleashed chaos of energy.

BUCKMINSTER FULLER

God doesn't make orange juice;
God makes oranges.

JESSE JACKSON

At the next vacancy for God, if I am elected,
I shall forgive last the delicately wounded
who, having been slugged no harder than anyone else,
never got up again, neither to fight back,
nor to finger their jaws in painful admiration.

They who are wholly broken, and they in whom
mercy is understanding, I shall embrace at once
and lead to pillows in heaven. But they who are
the meek by trade, baiting the best of their betters
with extortions of a mock-helplessness

I shall take last to love, and never wholly.
Let them all into Heaven—I abolish Hell—
but let it be read over them as they enter:
"Beware the calculations of the meek, who gambled
nothing, gave nothing, and could never receive enough."

JOHN CIARDI
"In Place of a Curse"

(Whenever I'm asked what I'd do if I could play God, I always think of this fierce mix of affirmation and admonition, which can be placed alongside the beatitude that says the meek shall inherit the earth.)

Every morning when I wake
      dear Lord a little prayer I make
O please to keep thy lovely eye
      on all poor creatures born to die

And every evening at sundown I ask
      blessing on the town
for whether we last the night or no
      I'm sure is always touch and go

DYLAN THOMAS
"Reverend Eli Jenkins"

(This simple, lovely childlike prayer was stitched into an old-fashioned sampler by a friend of long ago. Framed, it graced the wall of our family dining room. Later, it hung for many years in my study. And now it hangs on the wall of my oldest son's kitchen. It is still the prayer the child in me makes, morning and night.)

i thank You God for most this amazing
day:for the leaping greenly spirits of trees
and a blue true dream of sky;and for everything
which is natural which is infinite which is yes

(i who have died am alive again today,
and this is the sun's birthday;this is the birth
day of life and of love and wings:and of the gay
great happening illimitably earth)

how should tasting touching hearing seeing
breathing any—lifted from the no
of all nothing—human merely being
doubt unimaginable You?

(now the ears of my ears awake and
now the eyes of my eyes are opened)

E. E. CUMMINGS

(Whenever I am asked to offer a prayer on a public occasion, I tend to refuse. But if it's something I have reason to do—at a wedding, for example—I offer this poem/ prayer. Its spirit is inclusive, accommodating almost anyone of any faith.)

Divinity is not playful. The universe was not made in jest but in solemn incomprehensible earnest. By a power that is unfathomably secret, and holy, and fleet. There is nothing to be done about it, but ignore it, or see. And then you walk fearlessly, eating what you must, growing wherever you can, like the monk on the road who knows precisely how vulnerable he is, who takes no comfort among death-forgetting men, and who carries his vision of vastness and might around in his tunic like a live coal which neither burns nor warms him, but with which he will not part.

Annie Dillard
Pilgrim at Tinker Creek

John had
Great Big
Waterproof
Boots on;
John had a
Great Big
Waterproof
Hat;
John had a
Great Big
Waterproof
Mackintosh—
And that
(Said John)
Is
That.

A. A. MILNE
"When We Were Very Young"

*(If you live for a long time, as I have, in the Pacific Northwest, where it rains all
winter long, you cherish the feeling of being warm and dry and still out in the
weather. This poem expresses that sense of well-being. A child understands. In the
quest for God, when you find out there is nowhere God is not and that you are as
much a part of the universe as the farthest star, you have a sense of well-being not
unlike the child in this poem. That is that. I often recited this to my children before
a meal or at bedtime. It's not a prayer. It's a state of being, understood by a child of
six or sixty.)*

Annotations

This section is brief. Most of the authors quoted have appeared earlier in the book and their works have already been commented upon. Or else the sources are self-evident in their cultural value—such as Flaubert's novel *Madame Bovary,* the children's poems of A. A. Milne, and the peppery speeches of Jesse Jackson.

Since most of the quotations in this section have been in my journals and scrapbooks for a long time, I've had a difficult time formally acknowledging source and copyright. I'm simply not sure where I found some of them in the first place—such as the words of Buckminster Fuller. If you happen to know the original source of any of these quotations, please advise. I'd like to know myself, and I want to give proper credit.

EDNA ST. VINCENT MILLAY won the Pulitzer Prize for poetry in 1928. My introduction to her poems was stimulated by Dave Garroway, who ended his television program with the lines quoted in this section of the book. I wanted to know what else she wrote, and read her *Collected Poems* with great pleasure.

If for no other reason, BUCKMINSTER FULLER will be remembered for his invention of the geodesic dome. He was an architect, engineer, social critic, and creative genius, with a global view of human problems.

Even if I don't always agree with him, I admire JESSE JACKSON for his efforts to keep issues of poverty and racial prejudice on the front burner of American social concerns. No public speaker—especially in the political arena—can match the creative eloquence of his oratory.

JOHN CIARDI was the long-time poetry editor of the *Saturday Review* and a brilliant and witty essayist on the subject of poetry. His book *How Does a Poem Mean* remains a classic doorway into understanding poetry. He wrote poetry himself, translated Dante, and wrote several books for children.

If you are familiar with the poetry of E. E. CUMMINGS, you might think his name should be written with small letters (e. e. cummings). I thought so. But it seems that the publishing world manufactured the myth, largely because Cummings wrote his poetry in lowercase, a custom he picked up from the traditions of classical Greek poetry. E. E. Cummings was also a novelist, essayist, literary critic, and painter.

No-Thing

Consider the hackneyed distinction between an optimist and a pessimist: Viewing the same partially filled glass of wine, the optimist calls it half full and the pessimist calls it half empty. End of platitude? Perhaps, but carry it further: A realist, I suppose, would ignore the discussion and drink the wine. A recovering alcoholic would avoid the wineglass altogether. A nihilist would smash the glass and its contents on the floor. And so on.

Not to be missed when considering the adage is the usefulness of the concept of *emptiness*. The space where wine *is not* is as important as the space where the wine *is*. Not only is your view of *something* involved, but your view of *nothing* as well.

One sets off, defines, and enhances the other.

Another view: The glass should always be poured half empty, because the pleasure is not only in the drinking, but in the smells trapped in the space above the wine. The space does, in fact, have something in it, but another sense must be used to appreciate that.

Or take the matter of being alone, by oneself—the absence of company. It may produce a sense of empty loneliness or blessed solitude. It's all in how you view and use the space. An alternative sense of being solitary is possible.

Or consider the world of computers, which depends on the elegant simplicity of the yes/no, open/shut, plus/minus gate for the storage and flow of infinite information. What *is not* is equally important as what *is*.

Nothing, emptiness, absence, space, nonexistence, void, blank, open, and empty. These are all stalwart words providing balance to the ideas of something, fullness, presence, time, existence, valid, marked, shut, and full.

Many thinkers have emphasized that the quality of life often depends on what you can get along without. They conclude that the best things in life are not things.

There is a Buddhist teaching story in which a monk encounters a man who has spent his life looking for beauty and truth. "Have you found what you are looking for?" he asks. "No," replies the man. "Wonderful," the monk responds. "What do you mean by saying my unfulfilled search is wonderful?" demands the truth seeker. The monk replies, "I mean you still have something to look forward to."

Only an open mind still has room for new knowledge. What is outgrown and used up must be discarded to make room for what is yet to be learned. And much of the best thinking is done alone—in deserts, on beaches, in bed, behind closed doors. It is why we say we need to get away— to escape from clutter and busyness—to hear ourselves think. Thoreau said, "A man who has to go to the village to get the news hasn't heard from himself in a long time."

Reflection, meditation, prayer, contemplation, rumination are the words for the act of providing a surrounding of *nothing* in which *something* can take place.

The simplest thing, carefully considered, can become a window on the universe. And most of the universe is nothing.

In traditional Japanese houses, the walls are not cluttered with bric-a-brac or paintings, because the Japanese think the art becomes wallpaper after a while—unseen except as background. There is a single place set aside on a single wall for a single work of art that is changed from time to time according to the seasons. It's called a *tokonoma*. By placing something of beauty in the *tokonoma*, the art gets noticed and appreciated—purposefully attended to.

In the *tokonoma* in our home, at the beginning of January, we hang a Japanese scroll—a calligraphic painting of a circle made with a single stroke of the brush. It was made by Sesuo, head priest of Takuwan Temple in Kyoto, with an inscription in kanji saying, "Emptiness, an inexhaustible treasure."

I treasure it, because it reminds me of the yet unfulfilled possibilities in the next twelve months. It's a Zen greeting— Happy New Year.

Thirty spokes are made one by holes in a hub
By vacancies joining them for a wheel's use
The use of clay in molding pitchers
Comes from the hollow of its absence;
Doors, windows, in a house,
Are used for their emptiness:
Thus we are helped by what is not
To use what is.

LAO-TZU
The Way of Life, translated by Witter Bynner

Moments

    of   Silence

      are   part

       of   the

                   music.

UNKNOWN

The pause——that impressive silence, that eloquent silence, that geometrically progressive silence, which often achieves a desired effect where no combination of words, howsoever felicitous, could accomplish it.

MARK TWAIN

"Is there any other point to which you would wish
     to draw my attention?"
"To the curious incident of the dog in the night-time."
"The dog did nothing in the night-time."
"That was the curious incident,"
          remarked Sherlock Holmes [to Dr. Watson].

ARTHUR CONAN DOYLE

Silver Blaze

One cannot collect all the beautiful shells on the beach.
One can collect only a few, and they are more beautiful if
they are few. . . . Gradually one discards and keeps just the
perfect specimen; not necessarily a rare shell, but a perfect
one of its kind. One sets it apart by itself, ringed around
by space—like the island.

For it is only framed in space that beauty blooms.
Only in space are events and objects and people unique
and significant—and therefore beautiful. A tree has
significance if one sees it against the empty face of sky. A
note in music gains significance from the silences on either
side. A candle flowers in the space of night. Even small
and casual things take on significance if they are washed
in space, like a few autumn grasses in one corner of an
Oriental painting, the rest of the page bare.

For it is not merely the trivial which clutters our
lives but the important as well. We can have a surfeit of
treasures—an excess of shells, where one or two would
be significant.

ANNE MORROW LINDBERGH

Gift from the Sea

I have noticed that nothing I never said ever did me any harm.

CALVIN COOLIDGE

Annotations

MARK TWAIN, perhaps the best-known, best-read, and most thoroughly American author, is the pen name of Samuel Langhorne Clemens. I tried to work out a pen name for myself once. Nigel Morgenstern. No? How about Seven Van der Valk? No? For a while, in honor of Boutros Boutros-Gali, the head of the United Nations, I considered using Robert Robert-Fulghum. Never mind.

ARTHUR CONAN DOYLE took up writing to supplement the income from a failing medical practice. In addition to his Sherlock Holmes stories, which made him rich and famous, he wrote two other series of adventure novels. Doyle was a believer in and a devout supporter of spiritualism. The great American magician Houdini became Doyle's bitter opponent over Houdini's attempts to unmask the fraudulent claims of spiritualism and other occult practices.

ANNE MORROW LINDBERGH's life was lived in the shadow of her husband's flying achievements and the kidnapping and murder of her first child. Her letters and diaries, published in five volumes, were an attempt to set the record straight about that part of her life. In 1955 she published *A Gift from the Sea,* which is still in print. It has become one of those rare special cases in publishing— a small, word-of-mouth success that is so clean and true and resilient in spirit that it remains as fine a work of art forty years later as when it was first printed. In the 1975 edition—the twentieth-anniversary edition—Mrs. Lindbergh appended a reflective chapter that enhanced my sense of her strength and wisdom. Looking for the exact wording of the quotation, I was compelled to reread the book. It holds up—still sings—and stands alongside the writing of Annie Dillard and Thoreau on my shelf.

CALVIN COOLIDGE, thirtieth president of the United States, is often described as a political buffoon, but the biography by William Allen White, *A Puritan in Babylon,* says otherwise. I was assigned to do a term paper on Coolidge in an American history course in college and was surprised to find how warped the common view of Coolidge was.

Bene-Dictions

This book began because of a suggestion from Robert Bernstein: "Why don't you collect quotations meaningful to you and put them in a small volume, to benefit human rights work?" I accepted this little seed with all the naive alacrity of the Jack and the beanstalk story. Little did I comprehend that, once planted, the seed would grow into a living thing out of all proportion to its inception.

To put it mildly, the project got out of hand—gloriously out of hand. And to bring it to what is a somewhat arbitrary halt is frustrating—affirmatively frustrating—in that the problem is having too much good stuff. If I included everything I want to pass on to you, the volume would have become encyclopedic.

After the first pass through the journals and files and scrapbooks I've kept since age seventeen, I realized some narrowing of focus was required. Hence the theme stated at the beginning: Most of the quotations included are those I really wish I had written and have, in fact, found reexpressed in my own words in my own writing in one way or another.

Finally, the quotations had to pass through these screens: short, provocative, fresh, and useful. Therefore, standard and well-known sources were cut; long essays and long passages from plays were eliminated; and photographs, drawings, and comic strips did not fit in. Some hard choices were made.

The greatest reward of the process was mine. I got to climb the beanstalk as it grew. I reread texts and novels long held in high esteem. In many cases, the original pleasure was renewed. Conversely, I wondered how I could have valued some of the material I once thought essential to my thinking. I was inspired to clean out some of the junk in my intellectual drawer.

Along the way, I came across much that I had never had time to consider but which is not referred to in this collection. My personal beanstalk booty is a great pile of new books to read, a long list of new plays to see, and the lyrics of new songs to learn to sing. The beginning of a new book of keepsakes is already under way. It seems that there is a great deal to be learned after kindergarten.

What I thought would be quick work took three years. When I had all the good stuff gathered, I spent an interesting month trying to find some order, shifting things between piles, considering what they had in common, looking for the right word that characterized them. In this way, each chapter became a small book of its own.

After all the selections had been placed, there were some good words left over that didn't fit anywhere—except at the end of the book. Call them bene-dictions: Good words to leave you with. There is no annotation section after these quotations. Most of the authors have already been mentioned or are well known. And when you get to the last quotation, I trust you will understand both why I say it is a fitting final example of words I wish I wrote and why I'm content to let them be the last words. I'm not fool enough to try and follow William Shakespeare in the batting order.

"And the king wanted an inscription
good for a thousand years and after
that to the end of the world?"
"Yes, precisely so."
"Something so true and awful that no
matter what happened it would stand?"
"Yes, exactly that."
"Something no matter who spit on it or
laughed at it there it would stand
and nothing would change it?"
"Yes, that was what the king ordered
his wise men to write."
"And what did they write?"
"Five words: THIS TOO SHALL PASS AWAY."

CARL SANDBURG
The People, Yes

hey are not long, the weeping and the laughter,
Love and desire and hate:
I think they have no portion in us after

We pass the gate.
They are not long, the days of wine and roses;
Out of a misty dream
Our path emerges for a while, then closes
Within a dream.

ERNEST DOWSON
"Non sum qualis eran bonae sub regno Cynarae"

(Dowson was a nineteenth-century British poet. These verses are taken from his most famous poem, addressed to a lady named Cynara. Each stanza ends with the same line: "I have been faithful to thee, Cynara, in my fashion." Those lines were translated into Latin as a title.)

In the Garden

Eve bites into the fruit. Suddenly she realizes that she is
    naked.
She begins to cry.
The kindly serpent picks up a handkerchief, gives it to her.
"It's all right," he says. "The first moment is always the
    hardest."
"But I thought knowledge would be so wonderful," Eve
    says, sniffling.
"Knowledge?!" laughs the serpent. "This fruit is from the
    Tree of *Life*."

STEPHEN MITCHELL

Parables and Portraits

(Stephen Mitchell's many collections of poetry, wisdom, and inspiration are a model
for this book. His own writing is equally impressive—notably in the volume cited.)

Ripple

If my words did glow
With the gold of sunshine
And my tunes were played
On the harp unstrung,
Would you hear my voice
Come through the music?
Would you hold it near,
As it were your own?

It's a hand-me-down,
The thoughts are broken;
Perhaps they're better
Left unsung.
I don't know,
Don't really care.
Let there be songs
To fill the air.

Chorus:
Ripple in still water,
When there is no pebble tossed,
Nor wind to blow.

Reach out your hand,
If your cup be empty,
If your cup is full,
May it be again.
Let it be known
There is a fountain

That was not made
By the hands of men.

There is a road,
No simple highway
Between the dawn
And the dark of night
And if you go,
No one may follow
That path is for
Your steps alone.

Chorus:
Ripple in still water,
When there is no pebble tossed,
Nor wind to blow.

You who choose
To lead must follow,
But if you fall,
You fall alone.
If you should stand,
Then who's to guide you?
If I knew the way
I would take you home.

WORDS BY ROBERT HUNTER, MUSIC BY JERRY GARCIA
(A Grateful Dead song)

(I first heard this sung by a hundred thousand people at the end of a Grateful Dead concert in the sixties. I will never forget the gentleness of the singing, the haunting loveliness of the words, or the moment of silence at the song's end.)

Things never were "the way they used to be."
Things never will be "the way it's going to be someday."
Things are always just the way they are for the time being.
And the time being is always in motion.

ALEXANDER EVANGELI XENOPOULOUDAKIS

(Although the ideas in this quotation are old and contained in parts of many statements, they have not, to my knowledge, been set down just this way before. Alexander Evangeli Xenopouloudakis is a character in a novel-in-progress—mine. If you can't find the exact quote you want, make it up.)

Our revels now are ended. These our actors,
As I foretold you, were all spirits and
Are melted into air, into thin air;
And, like the baseless fabric of this vision,
The cloud-capped towers, the gorgeous palaces,
The solemn temples, the great globe itself,
Yea, all which it inherit, shall dissolve;
And, like this insubstantial pageant faded,
Leave not a rack behind. We are such stuff
As dreams are made on, and our little life
Is rounded with a sleep.

WILLIAM SHAKESPEARE
The Tempest, IV, i

PLAY

BELIEVE